KAFFE FASSETT'S
Quilts in Sweden

featuring Roberta Horton • Mary Mashuta • Liza Prior Lucy • Pauline Smith
• Brandon Mably • Sally Davis • Corienne Kramer • Judy Baldwin

A ROWAN PUBLICATION

The Taunton Press

The Taunton Press
Inspiration for hands-on living®

The Taunton Press, Inc., 63 South Main Street, PO Box 5506, Newtown, CT 06470-5506
email: tp@taunton.com

First published in Great Britain in 2011 by Rowan Yarns
Green Lane Mill
Holmfirth
West Yorkshire
England
HD9 2DX

Art director	Kaffe Fassett
Technical editors	Ruth Eglinton and Pauline Smith
Co-ordinator	Pauline Smith
Publishing consultant	Susan Berry
Patchwork designs	Kaffe Fassett, Roberta Horton, Mary Mashuta,
	Liza Prior Lucy, Pauline Smith, Brandon Mably,
	Judy Baldwin, Sally Davis, Corienne Kramer
Quilters	Judy Irish, Pauline Smith
Stitchers for	
Liza Prior Lucy quilts	Judy Baldwin, Corienne Kramer
Photography	Debbie Patterson
Flat shot photography	Dave Tolson @ Visage
Styling	Kaffe Fassett
Design layout	Christine Wood - Gallery of Quilts/cover
	Simon Wagstaff - instructions & technical information
Illustrations	Ruth Eglinton
Feature	Pauline Smith

Rowan Yarns: Patchwork and Quilting

Library of Congress Cataloging-in-Publication Data

Fassett, Kaffe.
  Kaffe Fassett's quilts in Sweden : 20 designs from Rowan for patchwork quilting / Kaffe Fassett.
    p. cm. -- (Patchwork and quilting book ; no. 13)
  Summary: "Kaffe Fassett presents 20 beautiful quilts that feature his trademark dynamic
colorways and patterns. Complete instructions for creating each museum quality quilt are included
along with tips and techniques that Kaffe has gathered in his more than 30 years of experience"--
Provided by publisher.
  ISBN 978-1-60085-401-9 (pbk.)
 1. Quilting--Patterns. 2. Patchwork--Patterns. 3. Quilts--Sweden. I. Title. II. Title: Quilts in
Sweden.
  TT835.F3677 2011
  746.46--dc22
                         2011012635

Colour reproduction by KHL Chroma Graphics Pte. Ltd
Printed and bound in Singapore by KHL Printing Co. Pte Ltd

contents

introduction

When I first visited Sweden in 1989 I was struck by the realization that so much of the urban architecture I had grown up with in America had a strong Scandinavian influence (the proportions of the porches, doors and window frames of the wooden houses in California were modelled by pioneer builders from Northern Europe). But the world was dazzled then by clean, modern Scandinavian design so it came as a very delightful surprise to see that their past was rich in the bold use of colour and pattern. Early Swedes revelled in painted furniture, murals on the walls and ceilings, and heavily carved doors.

All this is beautifully preserved and presented in the ambitious outdoor museum of period houses in Stockholm called Skansen. Unique and typical examples of dwellings from school houses and farms to grand townhouses and churches have been brought from all over Sweden to give the viewer a concentrated impression of the flare for decoration that existed in this country.

What a bonus it was for us (who are in the business of heightening our aesthetic surroundings by making our own beauty) to be able to take a truck-load of quilts to this rich community and be given *carte blanche* to display and photograph them.

OPPOSITE: A mural in the 19th-century Delsbo farmstead at Skansen, in rich reds and blues, by Eric and Anders Andersson of Ulvi.

OPPOSITE (BELOW LEFT): A panoramic view of old Stockholm.

OPPOSITE (BELOW RIGHT): The china kitchen in Skogaholm manor. The furniture was painted to resemble the china.

RIGHT: The drawing room in an 18th-century manor house, with the typical style of furniture and wall paintings.

BELOW LEFT: The intricately painted dresser and stencilled walls in the Delsbo farmstead.

BELOW RIGHT: The blue and white china kitchen in the 18th-century Skogaholm Manor.

When we decided last year to use this great outdoor museum as the location for this book I chose a palette for many of my quilts that would harmonize with the colours at Skansen. Hence the predominance in them of golden-brown tones and delicate pastels that would go with the classic Swedish blue and white elements.

The days spent wandering round this unique collection of houses filled us all with deep joy, seeing how lush a room could be where everything was hand-made with love and the desire to live with beautiful, instead of pedestrian, objects. I hope you find the settings for our new quilts as stunning as we did, and that you make a trip sometime to view these locations for yourself. In one day you can travel though history and experience the origin of Scandinvia's great design sense.

NOTE: *Skansen Museum recreates the architectural heritage of Sweden in a large open air site. Best examples of original Nordic buildings have been reconstructed so you can step back ointo the past, walk around the typical manor, town and farmhouses with their rich decoration and furniture of the different periods, and see people dressed in authentic period costumes.*

ABOVE AND OPPOSITE: Details of the buildings and furnishings at Skansen – a feast for the eyes and a great source of inspiration for designers.

BELOW LEFT: The Hazelius mansion, built of timber and faced with yellow panelled walls, is typical of the town manor houses found in the outskirts of Stockholm in the 19th century.

BELOW: My Parquet quilt shown against the door of Jakobsberg, a wing of the Hazelius mansion.

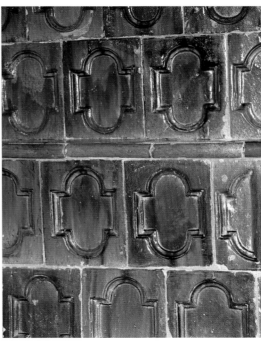

the fabrics

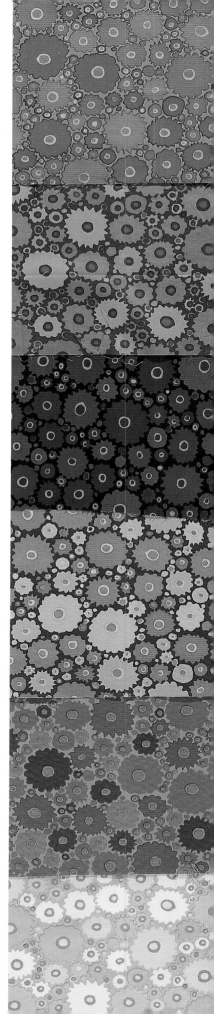

Plink by Kaffe Fassett (*far left*)
A primitive embroidery set my mind to this design of daisy like flowers. I have a passion for round motifs of different scales, so often produce circular designs that can be combined.

Rosette by Kaffe Fassett (*left*)
Another round floral, that was inspired by succulents that grow so abundantly in my native California. When I'd painted this out it reminded me of Rosettes that horsey girls accumulate from equestrian competitions, hence the name.

Cogs by Kaffe Fassett (*right*)
One of the favourite fabrics of people attending my quilt workshops was called 'Spools' and featured circular forms in different sizes. This is a new version of it in similar colour stories.

Radiation by Kaffe Fassett (*left*)
Another circular fabric to add to the collection of playful circles in different scales and two colour stripes that I love. The radiating stripes here give the print its name.

Ombre by Kaffe Fassett (*right*)
This fabric was requested by Kim McClean, a brilliant appliqué artist from Australia. She wanted a colour graduating print and this was my rather primitive answer to that request.

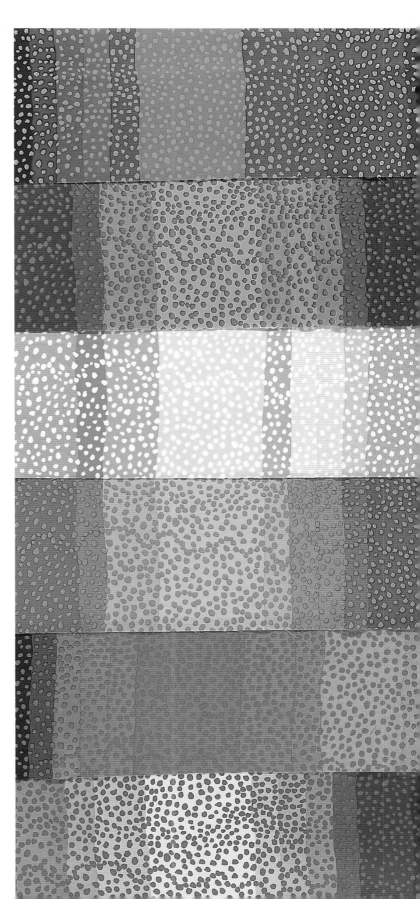

Shell Montage by Philip Jacobs (*below*)

The wonderful patterns on shells are boldly painted by Philip in this tapestry of a print. The subtle colours make it a useful print for many type of quilt.

Variegated leaves

by Philip Jacobs (*above*)

I've always loved geranium leaves when strongly patterned. They become a great addition to the circular motifs in a very organic way. I picked this leaf design from Philip's groups because I knew it would be a dream to colour. Which it certainly turned out to be.

Japanese Chrysanthemums

by Philip Jacobs (*above*)

Of all the many splendid florals Philip has resurrected from his fabulous archive this has to be my favourite. The great shapes of petals made this a joy for me to colour. It is proving to be as exciting to use cut up in quilts as it is as a stand alone print.

Pom Pom Dahlias by Philip Jacobs (*left*)
Yet another round flower that takes colour well. It is such an English chintzy like fabric that its really is a mood setter.

Primula by Philip Jacobs (*right*)
These little flowers have always charmed me. Amongst the first flowers to appear after the cold English winter. Each stem of blossoms is like a little bouquet. I enjoyed bringing my colours to these delicate blooms.

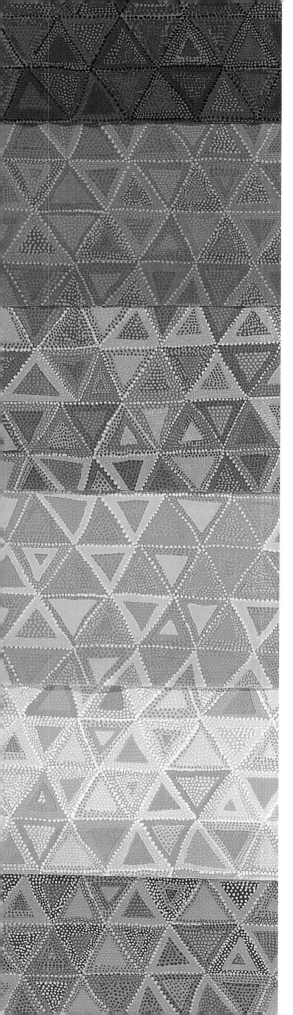

Beaded Tents by Brandon Mably (*left*)
In Brandon's collection of textile bits and pieces he has collected over the years is a leather strap, which he's sure was a belt from Africa once upon a time , decorated with contrasting coloured beads on a triangle pattern. The primitive placement of the beads, creating a contrasting dot, was a given idea for Brandon to try his own interpretation. He just loved painting this one out and doing the five colourways.

Herringbone Stripe

by Brandon Mably (*right*)
Stripes are always useful to cut up but Brandon wanted to break up the formality. He loves the markings of a filleted fish, chopped kindling for the fire, also his mother wore her hair in a french braid for years. All these images came together when playing with this pattern. Brandon would love to see this pattern used on clothing too.

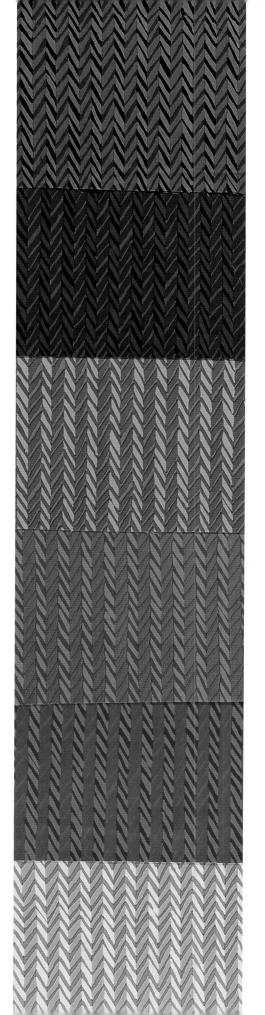

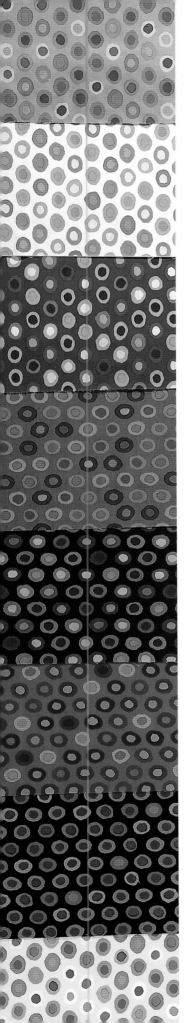

Rings by Brandon Mably (*left*)

A friend had an old shirt which Brandon just loved. Why? because of the simplicity of the pattern that would amuse his eye. It was made up of a three colour repeating circle with a contrasting dot centre. There was something so satisfying about the formality of this layout he had to play with it himself, but of course adding a few more colours. It reminds him of so many familiar household brands we see today like Cheerio's cereal, fruit Polo candies and even corn plasters. You could say inspiration is everywhere!

Python by Brandon Mably (*right*)

Although this comes from an organic source the pattern could have been inspired by islands or mushrooms which also have a rounded shape and form. Brandon really enjoyed adding a dot edge to the islands to resembling beading or scales. It amuses him to see how the fashion world seems to be embracing the same inspiration for this kind of pattern at the moment too. Plus it cuts up beautifully for patchwork.

Dancing Paisley

by Brandon Mably (*left*)

Kaffe introduced Brandon to the mesmerizing detailed world of the paisley patterns originally. But looking at the Liberty of London fabric archives he had a gut reaction of doing a swirl of large scale paisley - like a fantastic Vienna waltz in Grand Central Station. Once he started painting out the designs he broke up the striped bands with a contrasting dot to act like a sequin. Brandon's just tickled pink at how well this cuts up and works successfully with Philip and my fabrics.

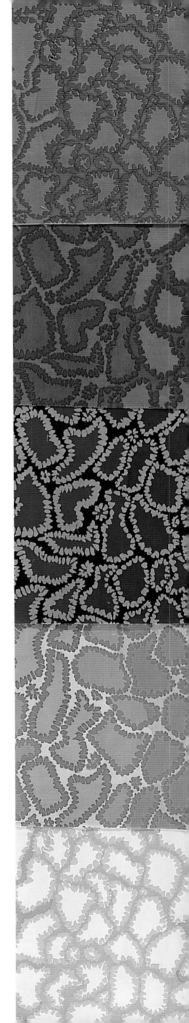

working with kaffe: *pauline smith*

When our publishing consultant, Susan Berry, first suggested that readers might like to know more about the way Kaffe and I work together on the designs for his quilts in these books, Kaffe was a bit reluctant. "People are always wanting to know what my secret is for designing my quilts", he said. "What they don't realize is I don't have a formula and hate the idea of colour rules and colour wheels!" This is because Kaffe works by eye. As he says, "I can't understand it in my workshops when people can't see which fabrics work as dark ones. The mistake is often because they look at the background colour rather than the overall colour. But it's dark if it's darker than the one next to it, not because it has a dark background." Where the placement of dark and light fabrics is important, for example in a Pinwheel design, this becomes a problem.

So we decided to take photographs at certain stages of some of the quilt designs with some relevant notes about decisions that were taken and changes that were made, so you could see the process by which Kaffe makes those design decisions. Here are a few examples of quilts in this book at the design stages followed by a bit of background information about the working relationship that has developed with Kaffe on this series of books.

SUNLIGHT IN THE FOREST

Kaffe took this simple layout to show off the large-scale fabrics to advantage. The largest block was determined by the size of the blooms in Philip Jacob's Japanese Chrysanthemum fabric in rich earthy shades. The next block size nicely fits around the hot red flowers cut from Kaffe's Embroidered Shawl fabric. More fabrics that seem to fit the mood are pulled off the shelves and heaped together on the floor. It's looking good. (Although I don't buy much equipment, I have invested in a large cutting square so as to be able to fussy-cut easily and accurately.)

stage 1 These are the first blocks roughly placed on the design wall. Kaffe always wants plenty cut before he starts the placement.

stage 2 Kaffe begins to make changes.

stage 3 Note how black Line Dance adds drama and balance to the composition. Magenta flowers add punchy highlights. Kaffe picks out light, medium and dark shades to create a dappled effect. "I like light trailing through dark areas, a bit like a Tibetan robe."

stage 4 More drama is added by the red blooms of Kaffe's Embroidered Shawl fabric. As Kaffe says, "This is the sort of fabric that looks flat in a big piece but when it's cut up it's gorgeous. I always design thinking about how the fabric cuts up." The two squares of black Line Dance in the centre have now been separated. As the eye was drawn to the large rectangle created. Notice how the same fabric cut into the smallest squares works when placed adjacently. Kaffe's Ombre fabric is perfect for the inner border. A simple pieced border of squares is all that's needed to complete this quilt. "I wanted the final border to merge so avoided using any of the dark fabrics."

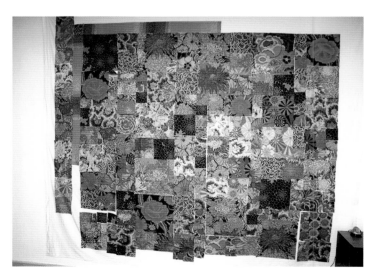

IMARI PLATE

This is based on an Imari plate Kaffe saw in a magazine. He thought it would make an interesting centre for a medallion quilt.

stage 1 This shows the quilt centre and the first stage of designing: trying out some possible fabric combinations.

stage 2 Trying out blocks, possible borders and different fabric combinations with lime Persian Vase fabric as an alternative to the pink Babble in the first pieced border. Sizes have yet to be worked out. The first star appears!

stage 3 The first very hurried attempt at working out the star block. I'm already thinking the triangular inset piecings are a step too far. For speed, we used the same blocks as the first pieced border for the four corner blocks. Looking through the progression of the quilt you can see how gradually the stars become less complicated.

stage 4 Note the changes to the plain borders. Kaffe decided the first border of Mirage Stripe was indistinct so he tried turquoise Spot, which looks much fresher and works well with the adjacent borders. Note the Mirage Stripe border is being pushed further away from the centre. The very pale Spot fabrics with white backgrounds give the quilt the light, fresh quality Kaffe wanted in this quilt.

stage 5 The lime Persian Vase is chosen for the first pieced border and also the third pieced border with blue Guinea Flower. The second plain border now needs to be changed as the apple Spot merges with it. Brandon's Straws fabric with its fresh pastel stripes is perfect and Kaffe tries it out as sashing between the stars.

stage 6 An additional border has been added before the star border in grey Persian Vase. This is cut so the star border will fit and also prevents the stars from merging with the previous border. Notice how the Mirage Stripe has disappeared and is replaced by Serape Stripe in pastel.

stage 7 Nearly there now! Kaffe just needs to decide on the binding...

STRIPED CITY

Kaffe wanted a simple, graphic quilt to show off his Serape striped fabric to best effect, rather like a large banner. Quickly cutting up large shapes of fabric makes me slightly panicky, there's nowhere to hide if it goes wrong. I'm also trying to calculate quantities, how to write instructions and how to explain it all to Ruth, who has the job of writing the final instructions and drawing the diagrams.

stage 1 Striped City is on the design wall. Kaffe and I felt we knew what we were doing with this quilt and could leave it at this point. I'm thinking huge in-set pieced triangles would be a nightmare to piece and was wondering how to proceed. We're already working on the next quilt, Dark Kites. Kaffe is ironing blocks and I'm cutting on the floor – my preferred workspace.

stage 2 Problem resolved! The large triangles are cut in half; no huge inset pieces in sight.

stage 3 (detail) Here is Striped City in close up. Note the way the stripes are joined. Some are deliberately mis-matched

---

CROSSES

An antique quilt that caught Kaffe's eye was the starting point for Crosses. He picked out the small-scale prints from the collection and Shot Cottons, mainly in subdued shades, with some spicy pinks and reds thrown into the mix (*see right*). To speed things up I cut large squares of different shades of Shot Cottons until we were satisfied with the colour combinations. The choice of black Plink for the sashing makes the perfect fabric to link the blocks.

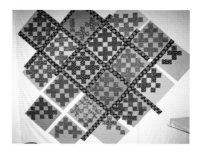

stage 1 The quilt is growing although the size and exact layout have yet to be established. The white markers indicate the blocks that Kaffe wants to repeat.

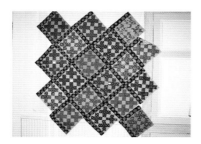

stage 2 Deciding on the width: with this layout you need a single block in each corner.

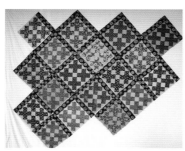

stage 3 This is a photo I sent to Kaffe for approval before the piecing was done and to plan how to finish the quilt. We decided to go for the simple option of Plink for the corners and outer border.

stage 4 Checking the corner fits.

BARCODE Kaffe used Serape striped fabric for a quilt based on barcodes. Other stripes are made from combinations of Shot Cotton, which were sewn and cut into sections. Then slices of different widths were cut: a great way of making the most from the fabric. The repetition of the stripes in varying widths gives the graphic, rhythmical look Kaffe was after.

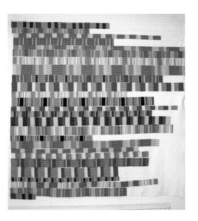

BEACHES This is another idea Kaffe had for Serape and Shot Cottons. He wanted to try cutting triangles in Serape and then arranging them to make interesting box shapes. For the boxes to work, it was important to cut the triangles with the stripes running along the base. Adding some odd boxes, made from different stripes, adds an unexpected dynamic to the design.

DARK ATTIC WINDOWS
stage 1 This photo shows the first placement of fabrics. The correct placement of the dark and light lozenge patches is crucial in this design to create the illusion.

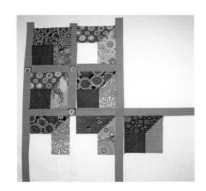

stage 2 Here the design is progressing. The border strip on the left is for another quilt: Dark Kites.

DARK KITES
stage 1 This shows the position of the pieced squares on point for before piecing. Brandon's Snakeskin is pinned on the left as a possible border. The Broken Dishes blocks need a dark and light fabric for the block to work. Some fabrics work as a light element in one block and a dark one in another block.

stage 2 This shows the large blocks of purple Babble. Kaffe is considering using red Snakeskin for the border.

stage 3 We thought the Snakeskin border shown in Stage 2 drew the eye away from the pieced centre so we worked out this pieced border. Because it didn't fit the quilt centre exactly we decided to add small rectangles of fabric at the ends of each border.

THE BACKGROUND

Kaffe selecting fabric

I am often asked how my work with Kaffe – making up his quilts for the Rowan patchwork and quilting series of books – came about and also what our working process is. So here goes!

I live in Holmfirth, in Yorkshire, close to Rowan Yarns' headquarters. Back in the '80s when my friend Stephen Sheard (the co-founder of Rowan Yarns) was looking for someone to make up a second set of quilts for display from the newly published book, *Glorious Patchwork*, which Kaffe had written with Liza Prior Lucy, he asked if I would be interested, as he knew I did some patchwork. I jumped at the chance, then panicked. This was a huge learning curve for me as I'd never seen, let alone used, a rotary cutter and ruler before, and some of the quilts looked complicated. I learnt as I worked and enjoyed the challenge, telling myself, "You can do it, it's just common sense and geometry". Afterwards, I couldn't believe I had cut with scissors for all those years.

When the first collection of fabric designs by Kaffe was produced, Kaffe was itching to start cutting them up and work out the many ideas he had buzzing in his head. So when Stephen asked if I would like to work with Kaffe at the Rowan mill, I didn't need asking twice. This was new territory for me and quite daunting. It was the first time I'd worked with anyone else on quilting projects, let alone Kaffe. I needn't have worried. He's an excellent communicator, talking me through his ideas, clearly explaining what he wanted me to cut, and giving me time to work out the measurements needed to realize his designs. As the day wore on we mocked up sections of quilts. My homework was to continue cutting and piecing blocks so that on his return visit he could decide on the final placement. This is how he also works with Liza Prior-Lucy in America. Some of the designs I did with him found their way into the first Rowan book alongside the ones he did with Liza.

Nowadays Kaffe comes up to stay in Yorkshire with me, allowing us to work out several ideas in just a few days. Such is Kaffe's enthusiasm to get going, he barely takes off his jacket before pulling out notebooks full of new quilt ideas, showing me his recent purchases of quilt books and his latest fabric designs. Often he's emailed some ideas in advance so we can hit the ground running. Other times, while travelling, he will spot a tiled floor or an antique carpet, and he quickly sketches the design on the back of an old envelope. Once in my workroom, Kaffe talks me through his design, explaining what he wants to achieve. Often he wants to showcase particular fabrics so the block size is important, especially when fussy cutting a floral fabric for example. He pulls out fabric he wants to use and I start cutting as fast as I can. We listen to the radio as we work (BBC Radio 4 is the station of choice in the UK for people like us working at home). My husband, Mike, brings us copious cups of tea along with slices of fruit cake at frequent intervals. Before long we're drowning in fabric. When there's no space left on the floor (where I do all my cutting) we have a fabric tidy. After lunch Kaffe has a short nap and emerges refreshed and ready to get going again.

We work out three or four quilt layouts in an average day. Some of these may be unfinished but will be left at a stage where I can carry on, having made notes on how to proceed. These are photographed on a design wall (I use a flannelette sheet) before being packed away ready for piecing. I will then email Kaffe photos of the quilt at various stage, sometimes with suggestions, for his comments or approval.

The view from Pauline's garden

Before dinner we usually have a walk across the fields, Kaffe drinking in the subtle colours and textures of the mossy dry stone walls he so loves. Some of you will know that *Quilt Road* was photographed in my house and the surrounding countryside. While I'm cooking dinner, Kaffe usually makes us a gin and tonic (very strong with lots of ice) and sits in the kitchen with his knitting or needlepoint. He's a pleasure to cook for and loves English puddings, his favourite being Sussex Pond Pudding. The evening is spent knitting, chatting, talking about books or watching televison – Kaffe is an X-Factor fan while I like Strictly Come Dancing – two of the most watched programmes on UK telly! Sometimes he disappears upstairs to take a fresh look at what we've been working on, trying out more fabrics to be included or swopped and making new fabric piles for cutting. What's so good about working with someone you get on with is the relaxed way discussions about family and friends, politics and the world at large just happen naturally. I am eternally grateful for the chance to work with Kaffe because I have learnt so much from him. When designing my own quilts I now know not to stick doggedly to first fabric choices, to keep an open mind, try all possibilities and above all enjoy the process. I hope this feature helps you to do the same!

Adding the last row of blocks to Rattan Squares.

Dark Windows by Kaffe Fassett

The painted cabinet and the pottery (*left*) are the perfect backdrop for the golds and rusts in *Dark Windows* which glow in the light from the window while (*above*) the strong geometry of *Dark Windows* looks great against the handsome woodwork of this loft.

Rattan Squares by Kaffe Fassett

This simple layout is a handsome way to showcase your favourite large scale prints. Brandon Mably's Babble feels to me like woven rattan, hence the name. I love it on this panelled door.

Parquet by Kaffe Fassett

The herringbone pattern of *Parquet* looks great on this beautifully weathered building at the heart of Skansen. I picked these warm wood tones when designing this quilt, knowing we'd find a perfect setting in Skansen.

Crosses by Kaffe Fassett

Crosses is inspired by a vintage quilt I saw. This quilt is so at home in this gorgeous painted room in Delsbo farmstead. I particularly like the chevron door to the right.

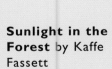

Sunlight in the Forest by Kaffe Fassett

One of the grander rooms at Skansen, which shows my *Sunlight In The Forest* quilt to advantage. I love the painted ceiling, pressed leather walls and jade-green bed. The fabrics in this quilt live up to the rich setting.

Dark Kites by Kaffe Fassett
Dark Kites is a dramatic but simple-to-construct quilt that looks stunning against the weathered red paint of Swedish barns.

Imari Plate by Kaffe Fassett

With a collection of classic blue and white china like this, who needs wallpaper? The cool pastels of my *Imari Plate* quilt shimmer in the cool Scandinavian light.

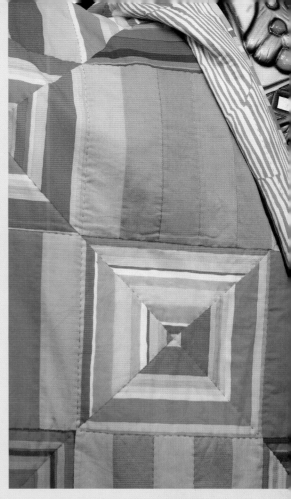

Beach by Kaffe Fassett

How lucky we were to discover this delightful carousel to show off my bold *Beach* quilt. Its rich palette is enhanced by the beautiful painted panels and coal-black horse. My Serape stripe comes into its own here.

Barcode by Kaffe Fassett

I have been obsessed with stripes
this past few years and this quilt
reflects that, and some! It was
inspired by interference on the TV
but then reminded me of barcodes
when completed. The bold painted
room in this farmhouse delights me
as a setting.

Striped City by
Kaffe Fassett

If I have to pick
a favourite use
of Serape stripe,
this *Striped City
Quilt* has to be
it. How at home
it looks against a
barn wall and on
these Swedish
horses!

Regatta by
Pauline Smith
Pauline's *Regatta*
has a deep charm
that is splendidly
enlivened when
pinned to this
puppet theatre at
Skansen. My Mirage
Stripe and Buttons
fabrics are
gorgeously
showcased here.

Vintage by Pauline Smith

This delicate pastel treat of a quilt, which captures the look of a vintage quilt from the 1930s, is so at home with the classic blue and white details that are typical of the Swedish aesthetic.

Shells by Liza Prior Lucy
Liza's *Shells* quilt showcases Philip Jacobs' popular Shell Montage print. The tones harmonize so well with the architectural details, like the panelled door and ironwork above.

Headlights by Liza Prior Lucy
The murals of the garden house became a dramatic setting for Liza's *Headlights* quilt.
Below we see a charming smaller kiosk at Skansen, a place rich in photogenic details.

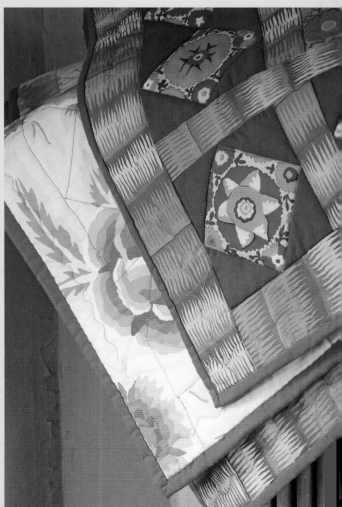

Romantic Shawl by Mary Mashuta

Mary Mashuta's celebration of a quilt, *Romantic Shawl*, plays so well with my stripes and circular prints. It's lined with my Embroidered Shawl print. Mary says the borders remind her of a beautiful vintage shawl or scarf, hence the name.

Illuminated Lattice by Roberta Horton

This dramatic quilt by Roberta echoes the equally dramatic floor in a classical Skansen drawing room. It is also shown to advantage on the dark wooden loft wall above.

Honeysuckle Afternoons by Corienne Kramer

Corienne's *Honeysuckle Afternoons* with its warm palette uses my Ombre print exquisitely to frame the squares. How at home its gentle tones are both in this room and against the carved decoration of the storehouse.

Diagonal Pathways by Judy Baldwin

The rich purples of Judy Baldwin's *Diagonal Pathways* responds so well to the deep painted surfaces of the Skansen barns. Bekah makes a charming border.

Reflecting Pool by Sally Davis
Sally has used Philip Jacobs' Japanese Chrysanthemum print gloriously in this cool blue quilt. I love the way it contrasts with the red lacquer of this oriental desk at Skansen.

Seahorse by Brandon Mably

Brandon's *Seahorse* quilt is the perfect vehicle to showcase his new collection of fabrics. The singing colours work so well against the rich red and sage-green tones of this Skansen building.

barcode ★
Kaffe Fassett

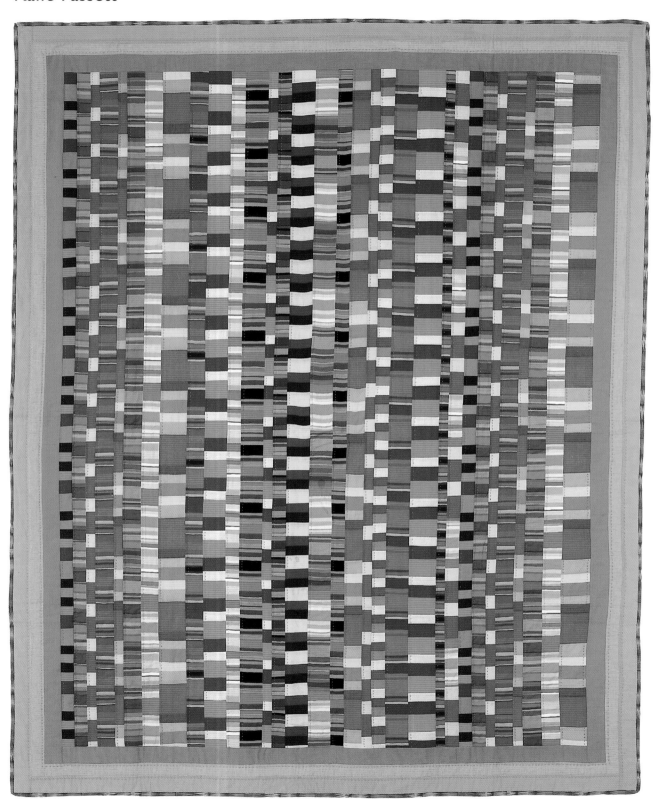

This is an easy quilt to make and is all about improvising and experimentation, creating your own stripes from Shot Cotton fabrics and using Kaffe's printed Serape stripe to make new and interesting stripe combinations. We have listed all the fabrics used in this quilt, but this is a perfect opportunity to experiment with your own choices. When cutting the Serape stripe fabrics use the photograph and column key as a guide, the trick is to use the same sections of the fabric together. For instance, in column 4 the broader sections of stripe are used, in column 23 the narrow sections of stripe are grouped. We have not provided a detailed quilt assembly diagram for this quilt as it is just a case of assembling a series of strips and 3 simple borders. Stay relaxed and enjoy the creative process!

SIZE OF QUILT
The finished quilt will measure approx. 69in x 89in (175.25cm x 226cm).

MATERIALS
PATCHWORK AND BORDER FABRICS
SERAPE
Bold	GP111BD	¾yd (70cm)
Green	GP111GN	1yd (90cm)
Pastel	GP111PT	1yd (90cm)
Red	GP111RD	1¼yd (1.15m)

SHOT COTTON
Thunder	SC06	¼yd (25cm)
Mustard	SC16	⅞yd (80cm)
Watermelon	SC33	⅜yd (35cm)
Lemon	SC34	⅝yd (60cm)
Apricot	SC79	⅝yd (60cm)
Clementine	SC80	½yd (45cm)
Magenta	SC81	⅜yd (35cm)
Lipstick	SC82	½yd (45cm)
Ice	SC85	¼yd (25cm)
Blueberry	SC88	⅜yd (35cm)
Honeydew	SC95	⅞yd (80cm)

BACKING FABRIC 5¾yd (5.25m)
We suggest these fabrics for backing
SERAPE Antique, GP111AN or Red, GP111RD.

BINDING
MIRAGE STRIPE
Red   GP104RD ⅞yd (80cm)

BATTING
77in x 97in (195.5cm x 246.5cm).

QUILTING THREAD
A selection of toning and contrasting perle embroidery threads.

CUTTING OUT AND PIECING
The centre section of Kaffe's quilt measured 58½in x 79½in (148.5cm x 202cm) to the raw edge. As this quilt is all about experimentation your version may turn out a different size depending on the strip sizes you cut, therefore cut borders to fit your finished quilt centre.

INNER BORDER Cut 8 strips 2½in (6.5cm) wide across the width of the fabric, join as necessary and cut 2 borders for the quilt top and bottom and 2 borders for the quilt sides in SC16.

MIDDLE BORDER Cut 8 strips 2in (5cm) wide across the width of the fabric, join as necessary and cut 2 borders for the quilt top and bottom and 2 borders the quilt sides in SC79.

OUTER BORDER Cut 8 strips 2½in (6.5cm) wide across the width of the fabric, join as necessary and cut 2 borders for the quilt top and bottom and 2 borders for the quilt sides in SC95.

QUILT CENTRE COLUMNS
Cut the Shot Cotton fabrics across the width of the fabric. The strip widths vary from 1½in to 4in (3.75cm to 10.25cm) wide, we have not specified the individual strip sizes for each colour, but the column key gives an indication of the proportions. Refer to the column key for the fabric combination for each column. You will notice that some combinations are repeated several times, for example columns 5, 8, 18, 29 and 32.

Using a ¼in (6mm) seam allowance throughout piece the strips into strip sets as shown in diagram a. Cut sections as shown in diagrams b and c and piece end to end into columns as shown in diagrams d and e. The cut sizes of the columns vary from 1½in to 3½in (3.75cm to 9cm), again we have not specified the individual column sizes, but the column key will give an indication of the proportions. In each case cut enough sections of the same width to make a column approx. 80in (203cm) long.

The stripes of the Serape fabrics are printed across the width, therefore cut sections across the width of the Serape fabrics varying from 3½in to 13in (9cm to 33cm) referring to the photograph and column key. Cut the sections into strips as shown in diagram f and g. Piece the strips end to end as shown in diagrams h and i to form columns approx. 80in (203cm) long.

TIP BOX
You will notice that there is a rogue column (24) where Kaffe decided to mix Shot Cottons with Serape fabrics, go ahead and have fun, it's what makes Kaffe's quilts sparkle.

COLUMN ASSEMBLY DIAGRAM - SERAPE

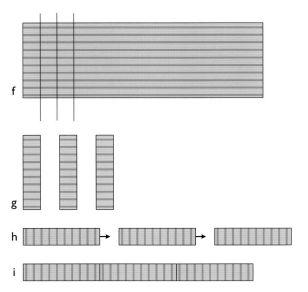

BINDING Cut 9 strips 2¹⁄₂in (6.5cm) across the width of the fabric in GP104RD.

BACKING Cut 2 pieces 39in x 97in (99cm x 246.5cm) in backing fabric. Seam the backing pieces using a ¹⁄₄in (6mm) seam allowance to form a piece approx. 77in x 97in (195.5cm x 246.5cm). Adjust these measurements as necessary to make a backing approx. 8in (20.5cm) larger than your finished quilt top.

MAKING THE QUILT

Join the columns to form the quilt centre. When sewing the columns together sew the first seam top to bottom, the second from bottom to top and so on. This will help to prevent distortion. Trim the quilt length evenly so the quilt centre measures approx. 58¹⁄₂in x 79¹⁄₂in (148.5cm x 202cm), but don't worry if the width of yours is different, you can add extra columns or leave some out as you please. Add the inner borders, top and bottom first, then sides. Add the middle and outer borders in the same way to complete the quilt.

FINISHING THE QUILT

Press the quilt top. Layer the quilt top, batting and backing and baste together (see page 140). Using perle embroidery threads quilt a line in each column, offset from the left hand seam by ¹⁄₄in (6mm). In the middle and outer borders quilt a line offset by ¹⁄₄in (6mm) from the inner seam in each. Trim the quilt edges and attach the binding (see page 141).

COLUMN ASSEMBLY DIAGRAM - SHOT COTTONS

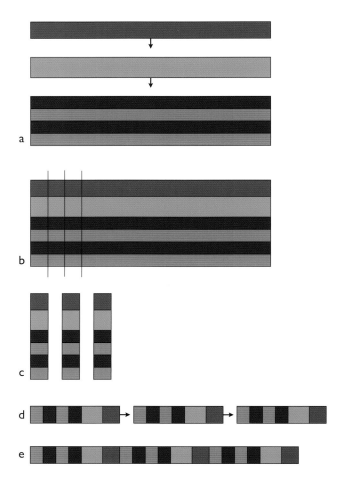

COLUMN KEY

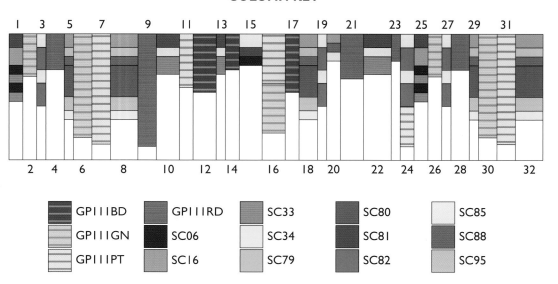

GP111BD	GP111RD	SC33	SC80	SC85
GP111GN	SC06	SC34	SC81	SC88
GP111PT	SC16	SC79	SC82	SC95

seahorse ★★
Brandon Mably

This quilt is made using a single triangle patch shape (Template O). The contrasting triangles are pieced into squares and joined into rectangular blocks which finish to 12in x 18in (30.5cm x 45.75cm). Brandon's clever use of colour means that each block has a seahorse shape against a vibrant background. The blocks are joined into vertical columns which are interspaced and surrounded by sashing strips to complete the quilt.

SIZE OF QUILT
The finished quilt will measure approx. 72in x 76in (183cm x 193cm).

MATERIALS
PATCHWORK FABRICS
FISHLIPS
Purple	BM07PU	½yd (45cm)
Rusty	BM07RU	½yd (45cm)

SPLASH
Brown	BM09BR	½yd (45cm)
Charcoal	BM09CC	½yd (45cm)

BABBLE
Charcoal	BM13CC	½yd (45cm)
Red	BM13RD	¼yd (25cm)

SHELLSCAPE
Charcoal	BM14CC	¼yd (25cm)
Red	BM14RD	½yd (45cm)

RINGS
Black	BM15BK	¾yd (70cm)
Green	BM15GN	½yd (45cm)
Red	BM15RD	½yd (45cm)

PYTHON
Black	BM16BK	¾yd (70cm)
Blue	BM16BL	¾yd (70cm)

SUZANI
Black	GP105BK	½yd (45cm)

SASHING FABRICS
STRAWS
Grey	BM08GY	1yd (90cm)
Lime	BM08LM	⅜yd (35cm)

BACKING FABRIC 5yds (4.6m)
We suggest these fabrics for backing
RINGS Red, BM15RD
SUZANI Black, GP105BK
BABBLE Red, BM13RD

BINDING
DAPPLE
Red	BM05RD	⅝yd (60cm)

BATTING
80in x 84in (203cm x 213.5cm).

QUILTING THREAD
Toning machine quilting thread.

TEMPLATES

O

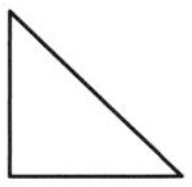

CUTTING OUT
TEMPLATE O Cut 6⅞in (17.5cm) strips across the width of the fabric. Each strip will give you 10 patches per full width. Cut 30 in BM16BK, 24 in BM15BK, BM16BL, 20 in BM09BR, BM14RD, 18 in BM07RU, BM09CC, BM15GN, 16 in BM15RD, 12 in BM07PU, BM13CC, GP105BK, 10 in BM14CC and 6 in BM13RD. Total 240 triangles.

SASHING Cut 2½in (6.5cm) strips across the width of the fabric. Cut 12 strips in BM08GY and 4 strips in BM08LM. Join the strips as necessary and cut 6 strips 2½in x 72½in (6.5cm x 184.25cm) in BM08GY, 4 for vertical sashing and 2 for horizontal sashing (in effect top and bottom borders), also cut 2 strips 2½in x 72½in (6.5cm x 184.25cm) in BM08LM for vertical sashing.

BINDING Cut 8 strips 2½in (6.5cm) across the width of the fabric in BM05RD.

BACKING Cut 2 pieces 40in x 84in (101.5cm x 213.5) in backing fabric.

MAKING THE QUILT
Use a ¼in (6mm) seam allowance throughout and use the quilt assembly diagram as a guide to fabric placement. First piece the template O triangles into squares as shown in block assembly diagram a, handle the triangles carefully as the edges are bias cut. Next arrange the pieced

BLOCK ASSEMBLY DIAGRAMS

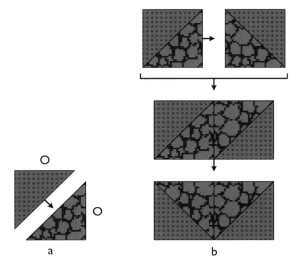

O

O

a

b

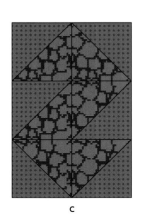

c

squares into the seahorse blocks and piece a total of 20 blocks as shown in diagram b, the finished seahorse block in shown in diagram c. Piece the blocks into 5 vertical columns of 4 blocks each. Join the columns, interspacing them with the sashing strips as shown in the quilt assembly diagram. Finally add the top and bottom sashing strips to complete the quilt.

FINISHING THE QUILT

Press the quilt top. Seam the backing pieces using a ¼in (6mm) seam allowance to form a piece approx. 80in x 84in (203cm x 213.5cm). Layer the quilt top, batting and backing and baste together (see page 140). Using toning machine quilting thread quilt in the ditch along all the sashing seams, then quilt in the ditch to outline each seahorse shape. Trim the quilt edges and attach the binding (see page 141).

QUILT ASSEMBLY DIAGRAM

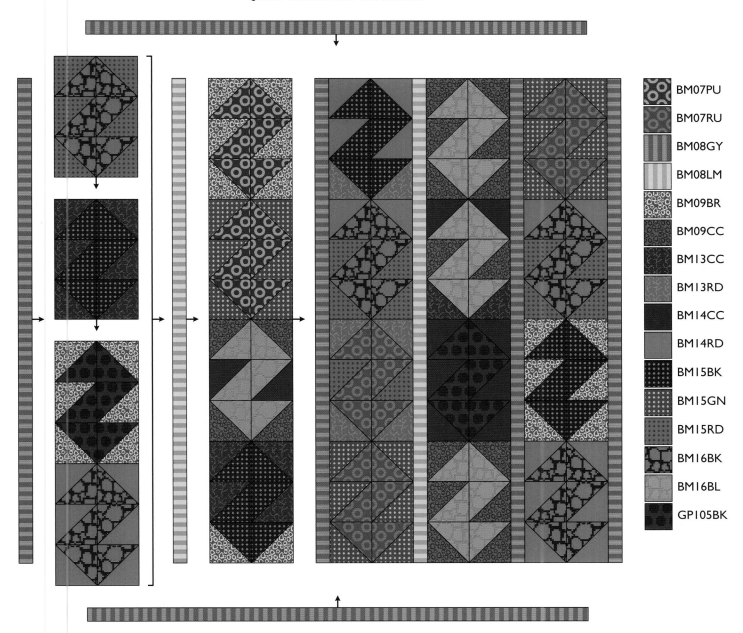

BM07PU
BM07RU
BM08GY
BM08LM
BM09BR
BM09CC
BM13CC
BM13RD
BM14CC
BM14RD
BM15BK
BM15GN
BM15RD
BM16BK
BM16BL
GP105BK

striped city ★★

Kaffe Fassett

This striking quilt is made using squares and rectangles of fabric (cut to size) with some careful matching and mis-matching of stripes which is important to capture the essence of the design. The pieces are joined into sections and then trimmed to produce the 45 degree angles, making the final assembly quite easy. Please review the whole instruction to understand how the quilt is constructed before you start cutting fabrics. We have allowed generous quantities of the fabrics to allow for matching as appropriate.

SIZE OF QUILT
The finished quilt will measure approx. 73in x 80¼in (185.5cm x 204cm).

MATERIALS
PATCHWORK FABRICS
SERAPE
Antique   GP111AN   1⅜yd (1.3m)
Bold   GP111BD   2⅝yd (2.4m)
Red   GP111RD   3¾yd (3.4m)
WOVEN MULTI STRIPE
Red   WMSRD   ½yd (45cm)

BACKING FABRIC 5¼ yd (4.8m)
We suggest these fabrics for backing
SPOT Black, GP70BK
RINGS Blue, BM15BL
DANCING PAISLEY Black BM22BK

BINDING FABRIC
WRINKLE
Purple   BM18PU   ⅝yd (60cm)

BATTING
80in x 88in (203cm x 223.5cm).

QUILTING THREAD
Contrasting perle embroidery threads.

CUTTING OUT
Please read all the cutting instructions carefully before you start. Use the photograph and stripe alignment diagram as a guide to cutting strips, which should match except where indicated (don't worry about matching the diagonal seams, these are random). Cut strips across the width of the fabric unless otherwise stated.

PIECE 1 Cut 4 squares 5⅛ in x 5⅛ in (13cm x 13cm) in WMSRD.

PIECE 2 Cut 4 rectangles 6in x 10⅝in (15.25cm x 27cm) in GP111RD.

PIECE 3 Cut 4 rectangles 8½in x 18⅝in (21.5cm x 47.25cm) in GP111AN.

PIECE 4 Cut 4 rectangles 10in x 28⅛ in (25.5cm x 71.5cm) in GP111BD.

PIECE 5 Cut 4 rectangles 9¾in x 37⅜in (24.75cm x 95cm) in GP111RD.

PIECE 6 Cut 2 rectangles down the length of the fabric 4¾in x 17in (12cm x 43.25cm) in WMSRD.

PIECE 7 Cut 2 rectangles 6in x 28in (15.25cm x 71cm) in GP111RD.

PIECE 8 Cut 4 rectangles 8½in x 22¼in (21.5cm x 56.5cm) in GP111AN.

PIECE 9 Cut 4 rectangles 10in x 31¾in (25.5cm x 80.75cm) in GP111BD.

PIECE 10 Cut 2 rectangles 9¾in x 40in (24.75cm x 101.5cm) in GP111RD.

PIECE 11 Cut 4 rectangles 9¾in x 21¼in (24.75cm x 54cm) in GP111RD.

BINDING Cut 8 strips 2½in (6.5cm) across the width of the fabric in BM18PU.

BACKING Cut 2 pieces 40in x 88in (101.5cm x 223.5cm) in backing fabric.

MAKING THE SECTIONS
Use a ¼in (6mm) seam allowance throughout and use the various diagrams as a guide to fabric placement. Make 2 sections as shown in section assembly diagram a, then make 2 more mirror images, total 4 sections. Trim the sections as shown in diagram b to remove the excess fabric, a trimmed section is shown in diagram c. Make 1 section as shown in diagram d, then make another mirror image of it for the opposite side of the quilt. Trim them as shown in diagram e to remove the excess fabric. The trimmed version is shown in diagram f.

SECTION ASSEMBLY DIAGRAM (continued overleaf)

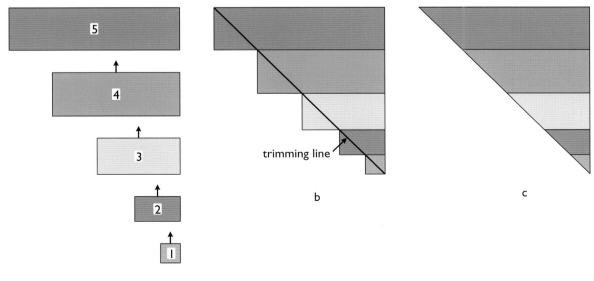

trimming line

a

b

c

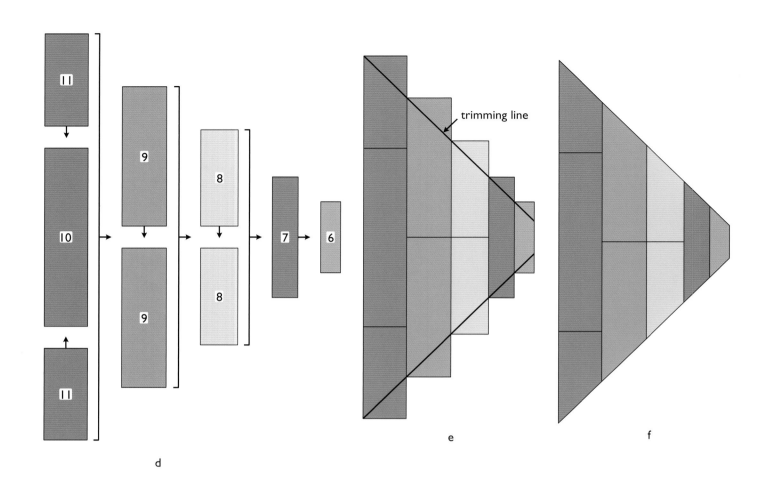

d

e

f

trimming line

QUILT ASSEMBLY DIAGRAM

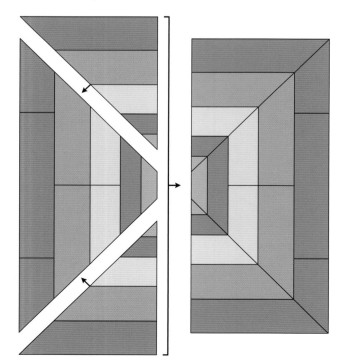

MAKING THE QUILT
Join the sections as shown in the quilt assembly diagram to complete the quilt.

FINISHING THE QUILT
Press the quilt top. Seam the backing pieces using a ¼in (6mm) seam allowance to form a piece approx. 80in x 88in (203cm x 223.5cm). Layer the quilt top, batting and backing and baste together (see page 140). Using contrasting perle embroidery threads hand quilt following the stripes in the fabrics in a series of 'boxes' working from the centre out approx. 1in to 2in (2.5cm to 5cm) apart. Trim the quilt edges and attach the binding (see page 141).

SECTION ASSEMBLY DIAGRAM

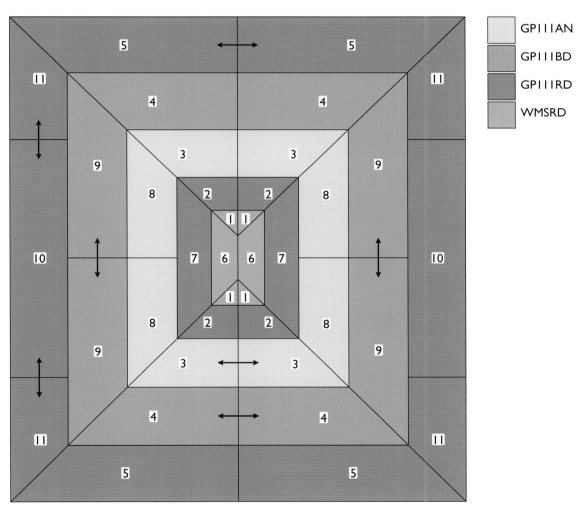

GP111AN
GP111BD
GP111RD
WMSRD

⟵⟶ Shows where stripes are mis-matched.

69

regatta ★★
Pauline Smith

The centre and borders of this quilt are pieced from a selection of rectangles, cut to size. Pauline wanted a portable, simple project so hand appliquéd the sailing boats to backgrounds, some of which were pre–pieced. She cut her boats and sails by eye and deliberately kept the 'points' of the sails blunt. We have provided example templates for the boat and sail appliqués as a starting point, trim and vary them as you please. When the appliqué is completed the rectangles are pieced into 5 columns which are joined to form the quilt centre. The quilt is finished with a pieced border. We have allowed a generous quantity of Serape GP111GN fabric so that the stripes can be used exactly as Pauline did, the longer border rectangles were pieced to match the stripes.

SIZE OF QUILT
The finished quilt will measure approx. 55½in x 55in (141cm x 140cm).

> **TIP BOX**
> When doing hand appliqué Pauline recommends dampening the fabric and finger pressing the seam allowances before pinning the shapes and stitching into place.

MATERIALS
Patchwork, Border and Appliqué Fabrics
STRAWS
Lime   BM08LM ¼yd (25cm)
SPOT
Lavender   GP70LV ¼yd (25cm)
Sapphire   GP70SP ¾yd (70cm)
MILLEFIORE
Blue   GP92BL ¼yd (25cm)
BUTTONS
Green   GP101GN ¼yd (25cm)
MIRAGE STRIPE
Lavender   GP104LV ½yd (45cm)
SERAPE
Antique   GP111AN ⅜yd (35cm)
Green   GP111GN 1¼yd (1.15m)
SHOT COTTON
Jade   SC41 ½yd (45cm)
Lime   SC43 ¼yd (25cm)
True Cobalt SC45 ½yd (45cm)
Clementine SC80 ¼yd (25cm)
Lipstick   SC82 ½yd (45cm)
Cactus   SC92 ⅜yd (35cm)

BACKING FABRIC 3¾yd (3.4m)
We suggest these fabrics for backing
MILLEFIORE Blue, GP92BL
MIRAGE STRIPE Lavender, GP104LV

BINDING
MIRAGE STRIPE
Red   GP104RD ½yd (45cm)

BATTING
63in x 63in (160cm x 160cm).

QUILTING THREAD
Perlé embroidery thread in toning colours.

CUTTING OUT
We recommend drawing out the rectangles and appliqué shapes onto the fabric before cutting for the best fit and to prevent waste. Rectangles 9, 28 and 30 are pieced to achieve the longer lengths.

COLUMN 1

RECTANGLE 1 Cut 14in x 13in (35.5cm x 33cm) in SC45.

RECTANGLE 2 Cut 14in x 3in (35.5cm x 7.5cm) in GP70SP.

RECTANGLE 3 Cut 14in x 5in (35.5cm x 12.75cm) in GP101GN.

RECTANGLE 4 Cut 14in x 6in (35.5cm x 15.25cm) in SC43.

RECTANGLE 5 Piece scraps of SC80, GP104LV and GP111GN, then cut 14in x 3in (35.5cm x 7.5cm).

RECTANGLE 6 Cut 14in x 15½in (35.5cm x 39.25cm) in SC41.

RECTANGLE 7 Cut 14in x 7in (35.5cm x 17.75cm) in GP70SP.

COLUMN 2

RECTANGLE 8 Cut 5in x 8in (12.75cm x 20.25cm) in GP92BL.

RECTANGLE 9 Cut 5in x 42in (12.75cm x 106.75cm) in GP70SP.

COLUMN 3

RECTANGLE 10 Cut 14½in x 15in (36.75cm x 38cm) in SC82.

RECTANGLE 11 Cut 14½in x 6in (36.75cm x 15.25cm) in SC92.

RECTANGLE 12 Cut 14½in x 14in (36.75cm x 35.5cm) in SC45.

RECTANGLE 13 Cut 14½in x 3½in (36.75cm x 9cm) in SC41.

RECTANGLE 14 Cut 14½in x 6in (36.75cm x 15.25cm) in SC43.

RECTANGLE 15 Cut 14½in x 7½in (36.75cm x 19cm) in GP104LV.

COLUMN 4

RECTANGLE 16 Cut 3½in x 11in (9cm x 28cm) in SC41.

RECTANGLE 17 Cut 3½in x 10in (9cm x 25.5cm) in SC80.

RECTANGLE 18 Cut 3½in x 4in (9cm x 10.25cm) in GP70SP.

RECTANGLE 19 Cut 3½in x 26in (9cm x 66cm) in GP111GN.

COLUMN 5

RECTANGLE 20 Cut 14in x 11in (35.5cm x 28cm) in SC92.

RECTANGLE 21 Cut 14in x 6in (35.5cm x 15.25cm) in GP104LV.

RECTANGLE 22 Cut 14in x 4½in (35.5cm x 11.5cm) in GP101GN.

RECTANGLE 23 Cut 14in x 12in (35.5cm x 30.5cm) in SC41.

RECTANGLE 24 Cut 14in x 4in (35.5cm x 10.25cm) in SC92.

RECTANGLE 25 Cut 14in x 8½in (35.5cm x 21.5cm) in SC82.

BLOCK ASSEMBLY DIAGRAM

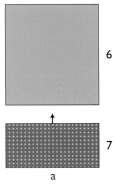

6

7

a

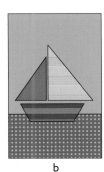

b

RECTANGLE 26 Cut 14in x 3in (35.5cm x 7.5cm) GP70SP.

RECTANGLE 27 Cut 14in x 4in (35.5cm c 10.25cm) in GP92BL.

LEFT SIDE BORDER

RECTANGLE 28 Cut 4in x 43in (10.25cm x 109.25cm) in GP111GN.

RECTANGLE 29 Cut 4in x 7in (10.25cm x 17.75cm) in GP70SP.

RIGHT SIDE BORDER

RECTANGLE 30 Cut 4in x 42½in (10.25cm x 108cm) in GP111GN.

RECTANGLE 31 Cut 4in x 7½in (10.25cm x 19cm) in GP70SP.

TOP BORDER

RECTANGLE 32 Cut 3½in x 17½in (9cm x 44.5cm) in GP92BL.

RECTANGLE 33 Cut 3½in x 5in (9cm x 12.75cm) in SC80.

RECTANGLE 34 Cut 3½in x 34½in (9cm x 87.75cm) in GP70SP.

BOTTOM BORDER

RECTANGLE 35 Cut 3½in x 36in (9cm x 91.5cm) in GP111GN.

RECTANGLE 36 Cut 3½in x 3½in (9cm x 9cm) in SC80.

RECTANGLE 37 Cut 3½in x 14in (9cm x 35.5cm) in GP111GN.

RECTANGLE 38 Cut 3½in x 4in (9cm x 10.25cm) in GP92BL.

APPLIQUÉ SHAPES

The example appliqué shapes on page XX do not include a seam allowance. Make card

or plastic templates, draw round the shapes onto the reverse of the fabrics, add a seam allowance of about ¼in (6mm) all around and cut the shapes out.

LARGE SAIL Cut 2 in BM08LM, GP104LV and 1 in SC82.

SMALL SAIL Cut 4 in GP70LV, 2 in GP104LV, SC80 and 1 in SC82.

BOAT Cut 4 in GP111AN and 3 in GP111GN.

BINDING Cut 6 strips 2½in (6.5cm) wide x width of fabric in GP104RD.

BACKING Cut 2 pieces 40in x 63in (101.5cm x 160cm) in backing fabric.

APPLIQUÉ

Refer to the Patchwork Know How

QUILT CENTRE ASSEMBLY DIAGRAM

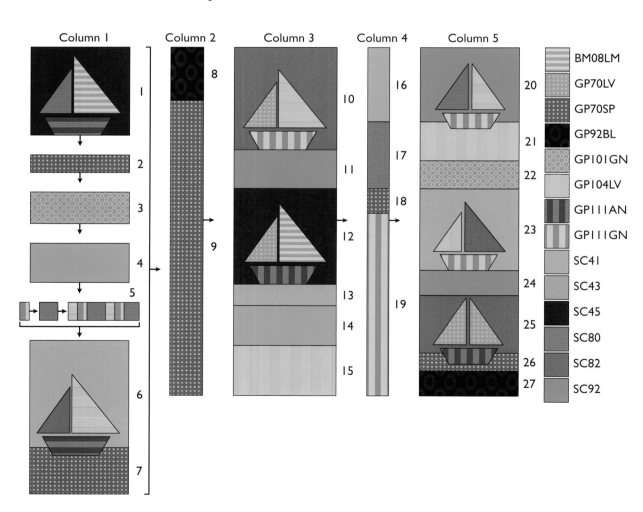

Appliqué section from page 139 for appliqué techniques. Prepare the appliqué shapes by finger pressing the seam allowances of the sails and boats except for the bottom edges of the boats for rectangles 1, 10, 12 and 23. Take the backgrounds for the appliqué shapes (pre–piece rectangles 6 to 7, 20 to 21 and 25 to 26 as shown in block assembly diagrams a and b) and pin the appliqué shapes into place. Where the boat 'sits' on the water (i.e. rectangle 1) align the raw edge of the boat with the raw edge of the background, the seam will capture the raw edge of the boat when the rectangles are joined. Appliqué the shapes to the backgrounds by hand.

MAKING THE QUILT CENTRE

Use a ¼in (6mm) seam allowance throughout. Referring to the quilt centre assembly diagram for fabric placement, piece 5 columns as shown. Join the columns to form the quilt centre.

ADDING THE BORDER

Piece the borders then add them to the quilt centre in the order shown in the border assembly diagram.

FINISHING THE QUILT

Press the quilt top. Seam the backing pieces using a ¼in (6mm) seam allowance to form a piece approx. 63in x 63in (160cm x 160cm). Layer the quilt top, batting and backing and baste together (see page 140). Using perlé embroidery thread in toning colours quilt in organic style in the 'sky' sections about ¼in – ½in (6mm x 12mm) apart to create a rippled effect. In the 'sea' sections quilt horizontal wavy lines in the style of waves. Quilt the sails lightly to prevent bagging. Trim the quilt edges and attach the binding (see page 141).

BORDER ASSEMBLY DIAGRAM

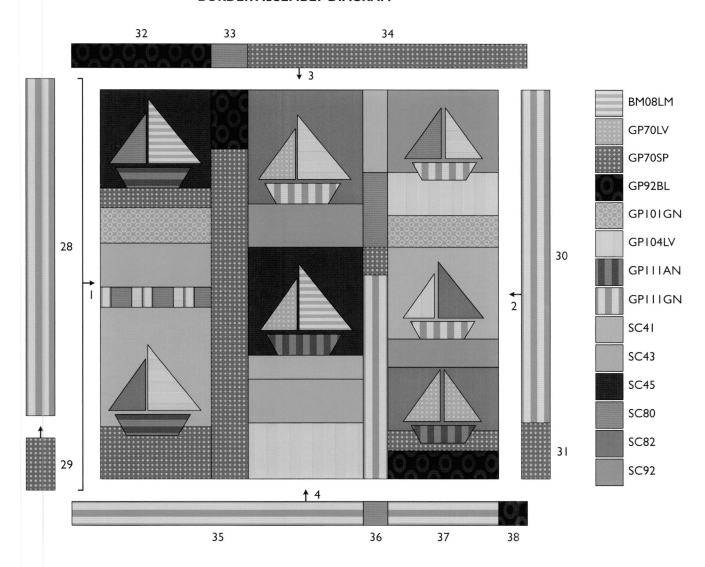

beach ★

Kaffe Fassett

2 block types (both finish 10in (25.5cm) square) make up this simple alternating design. Hourglass blocks are made using a triangle patch shape (Template L) taking advantage of the striped Serape fabrics to form interesting 'box' designs. The alternate blocks are pieced stripe blocks constructed from rectangle patch shape (cut to size). The blocks are pieced into straight set rows to form the quilt centre and then surrounded by a simple border.

SIZE OF QUILT
The finished quilt will measure approx.
69in x 89in (175cm x 226cm).

MATERIALS
PATCHWORK FABRICS
SERAPE
Green	GP111GN	⅝yd (60cm)
Pastel	GP111PT	2⅜yd (2.2m)

SHOT COTTON
Tangerine	SC11	⅜yd (35cm)
Sunshine	SC35	⅜yd (35cm)
Apple	SC39	½yd (45cm)
Jade	SC41	½yd (45cm)
Butter	SC64	½yd (45cm)
Pudding	SC68	¼yd (25cm)
Lipstick	SC82	½yd (45cm)
Pink	SC83	½yd (45cm)
Cactus	SC92	¼yd (25cm)
Sprout	SC94	¼yd (25cm)

BORDER BABRIC
WRINKLE
Blue	BM18BL	1¼yd (1.15m)

BACKING FABRIC 5¾yd (5.2m)
We suggest these fabrics for backing
SERAPE Pastel, GP111PT or Green,
GP111GN

BINDING
SERAPE
Pastel	GP111PT	¾yd (70cm)

BATTING
77in x 97in (195.5cm x 246.5cm).

QUILTING THREAD
Coats perle embroidery thread shade 433, Deep Turquoise.

TEMPLATES

L   Rectangle

CUTTING OUT
TEMPLATE L Cut 5⅝in (14.25cm) strips across the width of the fabric. Each strip will give you 6 patches per full width. Place the template with the long side along the cut edge of the strip, this will ensure the long side of the triangles will not have a bias edge. Cut 80 in GP111PT and 16 in GP111GN. Total 96 triangles.

RECTANGLE Cut 2½in (6.25cm) strips across the width of the fabric. Each strip will give you 3 rectangles per full width. Cut 2½in x 10½in (6.25cm x 26.75cm) rectangles. Cut 16 in SC41, 15 in SC39, SC64, SC83, 13 in SC82, 12 in SC11, 10 in SC35, 8 in SC68, SC92 and SC94. Total 120 rectangles.

BORDERS Cut 8 strips 5in (12.75cm) across the width of the fabric in BM18BL. Join the strips as necessary and cut 2 borders 5in x 80½in (12.75cm x 204.5cm) and 2 borders 5in x 69½in (12.75cm x 176.5cm).

BINDING Cut 9 strips 2½in (6.5cm) across the width of the fabric in GP111PT.

BACKING Cut 1 piece 40in x 97in (101.5cm x 246.5cm) and 1 piece 38in x 97in (96.5cm x 246.5cm) in backing fabric.

MAKING THE BLOCKS
Use a ¼in (6mm) seam allowance throughout and use the quilt assembly diagram as a guide to fabric placement. Using the template L triangles make a total of 24 hourglass blocks as shown in block assembly diagram a, the finished hourglass block can be seen in diagram b. Using the rectangles make a total of 24 pieced stripe blocks as shown in diagram c, the finished pieced stripe block can be seen in diagram d.

MAKING THE QUILT
Lay out the blocks in 8 rows of 6 blocks alternating the hourglass and pieced stripe blocks as shown in the quilt assembly diagram. Piece the rows and then join them to form the quilt centre. Add the side borders, then the top and bottom borders complete the quilt.

FINISHING THE QUILT
Press the quilt top. Seam the backing pieces using a ¼in (6mm) seam allowance to form a piece approx. 77in x 97in (195.5cm x 246.5cm). Layer the quilt top, batting and backing and baste together (see page 140). Hand quilt around the 'box' designs formed in the hourglass blocks, and diagonally across the triangles plus on both sides of the middle rectangle in the pieced stripe blocks using Coats perle embroidery thread 433, Deep Turquoise. Trim the quilt edges and attach the binding (see page 141).

BLOCK ASSEMBLY DIAGRAMS

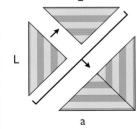

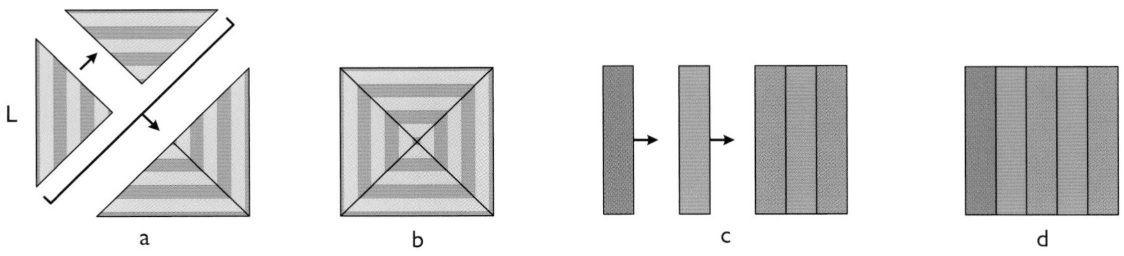

a

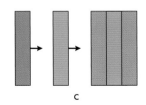

b

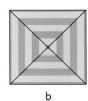

c

d

QUILT ASSEMBLY DIAGRAM

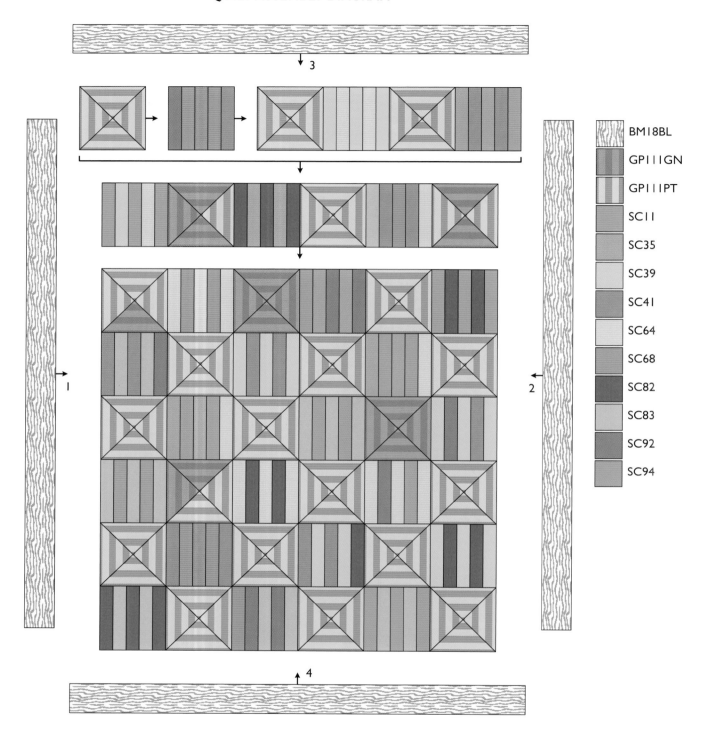

BM18BL
GP111GN
GP111PT
SC11
SC35
SC39
SC41
SC64
SC68
SC82
SC83
SC92
SC94

illuminated lattice ★★
Roberta Horton

This dramatic quilt is made from hourglass blocks (finish 6½in (16.5cm) square) pieced from 1 triangle (Template Z). The hourglass blocks are set on point interspaced with dark Shot Cotton sashing strips in 3 shapes (template AA, BB and Reverse BB and CC) and corner posts (Template T). The row ends are completed with half hourglass blocks. The clever graduated colour effect is achieved by careful piecing of combinations of fabrics working from the centre out. If you would like an even more dramatic quilt Roberta suggests using Shot Cotton Coal, SC63 for the sashing which is even darker! A design wall is very helpful for this quilt.

SIZE OF QUILT
The finished quilt will measure approx. 72in x 72in (183cm x 183cm).

MATERIALS
PATCHWORK FABRICS
BUTTONS
Green   GP101GN   ¾yd (70cm)
Pastel   GP101PT   ⅜yd (35cm)
SUZANI
Pink   GP105PK   ⅜yd (35cm)
EMBROIDERED SHAWL
Turquoise   GP106TQ   ⅜yd (35cm)
RUSTIC FLORAL
Kiwi   GP108KI   ⅜yd (35cm)
COGS
Blue   GP110BL   ¾yd (70cm)
ROSETTE
Pink   GP112PK   ⅝yd (60cm)
RAMBLING ROSE
Pastel   PJ34PT   ⅝yd (60cm)
SHELL MONTAGE
Grey   PJ37GY   ⅜yd (35cm)
POM POM DAHLIA
Pastel   PJ38PT   ⅜yd (35cm)

SASHING FABRICS
SHOT COTTON
Prune   SC03   ⅜yd (35cm)
Thunder   SC06   2¼yd (2.1m)

BACKING FABRIC 4¾yd (4.3m)
We suggest these fabrics for backing
EMBROIDERED SHAWL Red, GP106RD
ROSETTE Pink, GP112PK
COGS Green, GP101GN

BINDING
SHOT COTTON
Thunder   SC06   ⅝yd (60cm)

BATTING
80in x 80in (203cm x 203cm).

QUILTING THREAD
Invisible machine quilting thread.

TEMPLATES
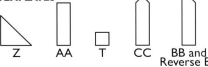
Z   AA   T   CC   BB and Reverse BB

CUTTING OUT
TEMPLATE Z Cut 5½in (14cm) strips across the width of the fabric. Each strip will give you 14 triangles per full width. Cut 44 in GP101GN, GP110BL, 36 in GP112PK, PJ34PT, 28 in GP108KI, PJ37GY, 20 in GP105PK, PJ38PT, 16 in GP101PT and GP106TQ. Total 288 triangles.

TEMPLATE T Cut 2½in (6.25cm) strips across the width of the fabric. Each strip will give you 16 patches per full width. Cut 61 in SC03.

TEMPLATE AA Cut 2½in (6.25cm) strips across the width of the fabric. Each strip will give you 5 rectangles per full width. Cut 120 in SC06.

TEMPLATE BB AND REVERSE BB. Cut 2½in (6.25cm) strips across the width of the fabric. Each strip will give you 4 patches per full width. In SC06 cut 10, then flip the template over and cut an additional 10. Total 20 patches.

TEMPLATE CC Cut 2½in (6.25cm) strips across the width of the fabric. Each strip will give you 4 patches per full width. Cut 4 in SC06.

BINDING Cut 8 strips 2½in (6.5cm) across the width of the fabric in SC06.

BACKING Cut 2 pieces 40in x 80in (101.5cm x 203cm) in backing fabric.

MAKING THE BLOCKS
Use a ¼in (6mm) seam allowance throughout and use the quilt assembly and fabric combination diagrams as a guide to fabric placement. There are 5 fabric combinations for the hourglass blocks, piece the blocks as shown in block assembly diagram a. The finished block can be seen in diagram b. Make 20 in fabric combination 1, 16 in combination 2, 12 in combination 3, 8 in combination 4 and 4 in combination 5, total 60 blocks. Make sure that the blocks in each combination are all identical as they are rotated in 4 orientations for the 4 sides of the quilt. Piece 24 half blocks as shown in diagram c.

BLOCK ASSEMBLY DIAGRAM

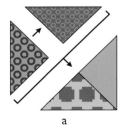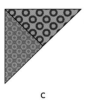

a   b   c

FABRIC COMBINATIONS

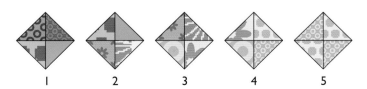

1   2   3   4   5

MAKING THE QUILT

Lay out the blocks in diagonal rows interspacing the blocks with the template AA sashing rectangles and template T squares. Fill in the along the quilt edges with the half blocks, template BB and reverse BB patches and the quilt corners with the template CC patches as shown in the quilt assembly diagram. Step back and make sure the orientation of the blocks is correct and the pattern is consistent. Piece the rows then join them to complete the quilt.

FINISHING THE QUILT

Press the quilt top. Seam the backing pieces using a 1/4in (6mm) seam allowance to form a piece approx. 80in x 80in (203cm x 203cm). Layer the quilt top, batting and backing and baste together (see page 140). Using invisible machine quilting thread quilt in the ditch along all the seams continuing across the template T squares at the intersections. Trim the quilt edges and attach the binding (see page 141).

QUILT ASSEMBLY DIAGRAM

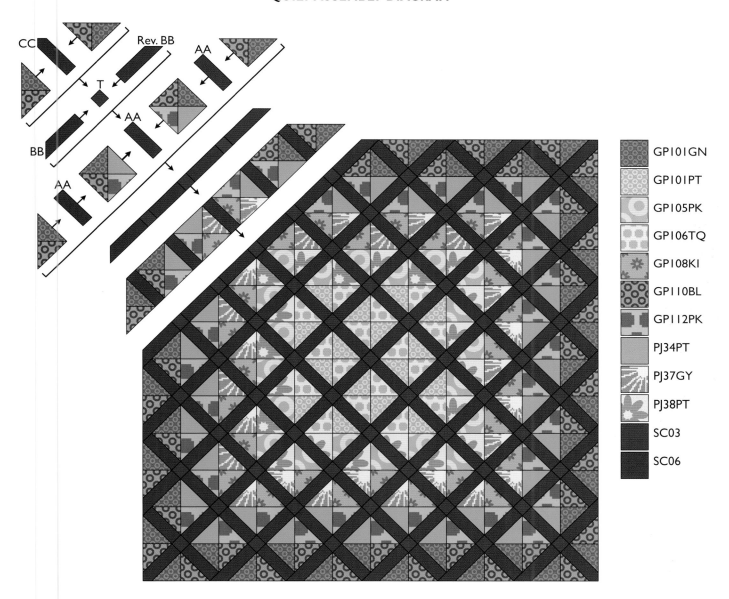

GP101GN
GP101PT
GP105PK
GP106TQ
GP108KI
GP110BL
GP112PK
PJ34PT
PJ37GY
PJ38PT
SC03
SC06

romantic shawl ★★
Mary Mashuta

The blocks for the quilt centre which finish to 10in (25.5cm) square are pieced using a square (Template H) surrounded with 2 rectangles (Templates DD and EE). The resulting pieced square is then set on point by adding a triangle patch shape (Template FF). The blocks are made in 2 colourways and are alternated throughout the quilt centre. The centre is then surrounded with a series of 3 borders. The inner border is extended into the middle pieced border which is made using fussy cut squares (Template H) set on point using 2 triangle patch shapes (Templates C and GG), the inner border is extended into the pieced border by adding rectangles of inner border fabric to the pieced border (Template HH) before pieced corner posts are added. A final border is then added to complete the quilt.

TEMPLATES

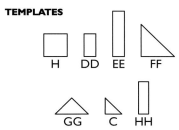

H   DD   EE   FF

GG   C   HH

SIZE OF QUILT
The finished quilt will measure approx. 67½in x 67½in (171.5cm x 171.5cm).

MATERIALS
PATCHWORK AND BORDER FABRICS
Extra fabric has been allowed for fussy cutting GP105RD.

MIRAGE STRIPE		
Red	GP104RD	1⅛ yd (1m)
SUZANI		
Red	GP105RD	1⅜ yd (1.25m)
PLINK		
Green	GP109GN	⅜ yd (35cm)
Magenta	GP109MG	⅜ yd (35cm)
COGS		
Green	GP110GN	¾ yd (70cm)
Red	GP110RD	⅞ yd (80cm)
SERAPE		
Green	GP111GN	¾ yd (70cm)
Red	GP111RD	¾ yd (70cm)
SHOT COTTON		
Viridian	SC55	⅞ yd (80cm)

BACKING FABRIC 4½ yd (4.1m)
We suggest these fabrics for backing
EMBROIDERED SHAWL Pink, GP106PK
PLINK Magenta, GP109MG
COGS Red, GP110RD

BINDING
SHOT COTTON
Viridian   SC55   ⅝ yd (60cm)

BATTING
75in x 75in (190.5cm x 190.5cm).

QUILTING THREAD
Toning and yellow machine quilting threads.

CUTTING OUT
Important Information
Please read carefully before cutting the stripe fabrics.
Stripe pattern placement is important to the design, refer to photograph and quilt assembly diagram if you are confused.
Open out the fabric and cut 1 layer at a time.
Use a gridded ruler to get the first accurate cut across the fabric by lining up the stripe lines with the ruler lines. Keep checking that your cutting line is accurate and take time to correct if necessary, the extra effort is worth it.
The stripes in SERAPE and MIRAGE STRIPE are printed in different directions, but both fabrics are cut so the stripes run perpendicular to the long edge of all the cut shapes. Cut the fabric as stated for the stripes to run correctly.

TEMPLATE H Cut 4in (10.25cm) strips across the width of the fabric. Each strip will give you 10 squares per full width. Cut 13 in GP109MG and 12 in GP109GN. Also fussy cut 44 in GP105RD centring on the designs.
TEMPLATE EE Cut 7½in (19cm) strips across the width of the fabric. Each strip will give you 17 rectangles per full width. Cut 26 in GP111GN and 24 in GP111RD.
TEMPLATE DD Cut 4in (10.25cm) strips across the width of the fabric. Each strip will give you 17 rectangles per full width. Cut 26 in GP111GN and 24 in GP111RD.
TEMPLATE FF Cut 5⅞in (15cm) strips across the width of the fabric. Each strip

will give you 12 triangles per full width. Cut 52 in GP110RD and 48 in GP110GN.
TEMPLATE GG Cut 6⅛in (15.5cm) strips across the width of the fabric. Each strip will give you 24 triangles per full width. Cut 6⅛in (15.5cm) squares, cut each square twice diagonally to form 4 triangles using the template as a guide, this will ensure that the long side of the triangle will not have a bias edge. Note: do not move the patches until both the diagonals have been cut. Cut 72 in SC55.
TEMPLATE C Cut 3⅜in (8.5cm) strips across the width of the fabric. Each strip will give you 22 triangles per full width. Cut 32 in SC55.
INNER BORDER Cut 6 strips 2in (5cm) wide across the width of the fabric, join as necessary and cut 2 borders 2in x 62⅞in (5cm x 159.75cm) for the quilt top and bottom and 2 borders 2in x 50in (5cm x 127cm) for the quilt sides in GP104RD.
OUTER BORDER Cut 7 strips 3in (7.5cm) wide across the width of the fabric, join as necessary and cut 2 borders 3in x 67⅞in (7.5cm x 172.5cm) for the quilt top and bottom and 2 borders 3in x 62⅞in (7.5cm x 159.75cm) for the quilt sides in GP104RD.
TEMPLATE HH Cut a 2in (5cm) strip across the width of the fabric. Cut 4 in GP104RD.

BINDING Cut 8 strips 2½in (6.5cm) across the width of the fabric in SC55.

BACKING Cut 2 pieces 38in x 75in (96.5cm x 190.5cm) in backing fabric.

MAKING THE QUILT CENTRE
Use a ¼in (6mm) seam allowance throughout. The blocks for the quilt centre are made in 2 colourways, refer to the quilt assembly diagram for fabric placement. Make a total of 25 blocks as shown in block assembly diagrams a and b, the finished centre block is shown in diagram c. Join the blocks alternating the colourways throughout into 5 rows of 5 blocks. Join the rows to complete the quilt centre.

ADDING THE BORDERS
Add the side inner borders to the quilt centre. Piece 2 side middle borders as shown in border assembly diagram d. Add these to the quilt sides. Add the top and bottom inner borders. Piece 2 more middle borders as before and 4 corner posts as shown in border assembly diagram e. Add

the corner posts to the pieced middle borders interspacing with a template HH rectangle as shown in the quilt assembly diagram. Add the top and bottom middle borders to the quilt centre. Finally add the outer borders as indicated to complete the quilt.

FINISHING THE QUILT

Press the quilt top. Seam the backing pieces using a ¼in (6mm) seam allowance to form a piece approx. 75in x 75in (190.5cm x 190.5cm). Layer the quilt top, batting and backing and baste together (see page 140). Using toning machine quilting thread quilt in the ditch between the blocks and the border seams. Using yellow thread quilt the blocks as shown in the quilting diagram and add a straight or decorative stitch down the centre of the outer borders. Trim the quilt edges and attach the binding (see page 141).

QUILTING DIAGRAM

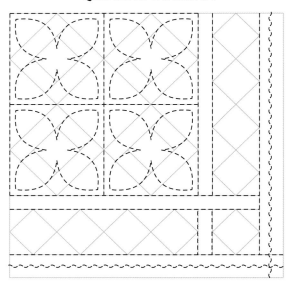

BLOCK ASSEMBLY DIAGRAM

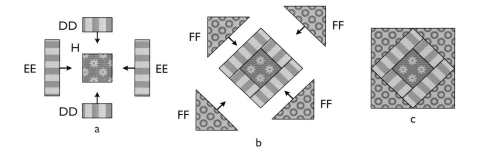

BORDER ASSEMBLY DIAGRAM

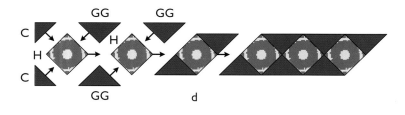

QUILT ASSEMBLY DIAGRAM

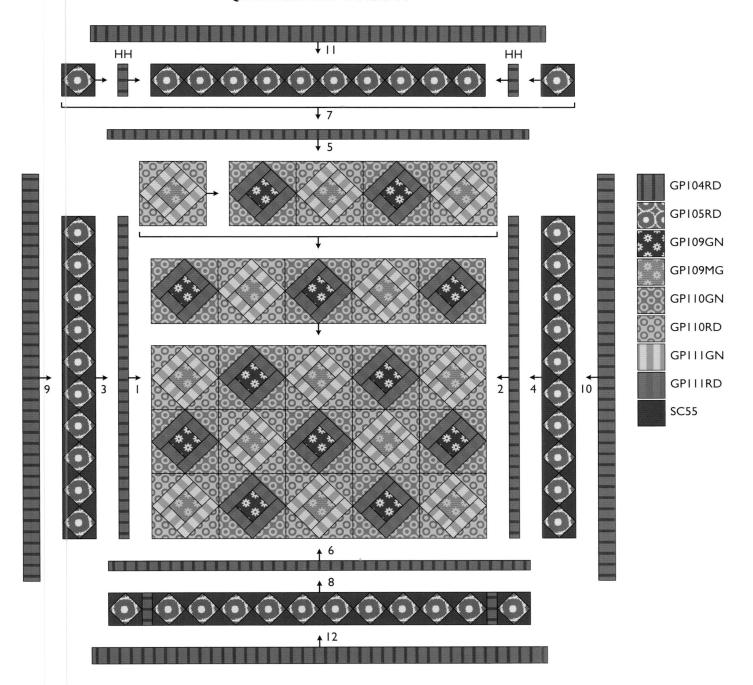

HH   HH

11

7

5

9   3   1

2   4   10

6

8

12

GP104RD

GP105RD

GP109GN

GP109MG

GP110GN

GP110RD

GP111GN

GP111RD

SC55

imari plate ★★★

Kaffe Fassett

This medallion style quilt is formed around an appliquéd centre square which is framed by a series of 5 simple and 4 pieced borders alternating out from the centre. The centre panel has an appliquéd design for which we used the freezer paper hand appliqué method, however it could be done by machine using fusible web if you prefer. It is embellished with embroidery.

The centre panel is framed with the first simple border (Border 1) followed by Border 2 which is pieced using a square (Template A) and a rectangle (Template B). These are pieced to make a small square block which is then set on point using a triangle patch shape (Template C). Please take care when cutting templates A and B as they are not a standard size and must be cut accurately using the template for the blocks to fit. Border 3 is simple, Border 4 is pieced using a triangle (Template D). Fabric GP60GY was used for only 1 triangle and GP70PE was used for only 2 triangles in the whole quilt, if you don't have a scrap of these fabrics substitute something similar. Fabric GP111FA is used for 16 triangles in border 4 which can be cut from a single strip, however Kaffe felt that the triangles were too uniform cut this way, so we have allowed enough fabric to cut these triangles from 2 strips to mix up the stripe patterns.

Border 5 is simple, Border 6 is pieced of 'square in a square' blocks using a square (Template F) and a triangle patch shape (Template E). Border 7 is simple but the fabric was fussy cut to match the design, we have allowed extra fabric to allow this.

Border 8 is pieced of star blocks using a diamond (Template G), a triangle (Template C) and a square (Template H). The blocks are interspaced with sashing strips (cut to size). Border 9 is simple and completes the quilt.

SIZE OF QUILT
The finished quilt will measure approx. 89in x 89in (226cm x 226cm).

MATERIALS
PATCHWORK AND BORDER FABRICS
STRAWS
Pastel   BM08PT   ⅞yd (80cm)
BABBLE
Pink   BM13PK   ⅜yd (35cm)
PAPERWEIGHT
Pastel   GP20PT   ⅝yd (60cm)
GUINEA FLOWER
Apricot   GP59AP   ⅝yd (60cm)
Blue   GP59BL   ⅞yd (80cm)
Mauve   GP59MV   1¼yd (1.15m)
PAISLEY JUNGLE
Grey   GP60GY   a scrap
SPOT
Fuchsia   GP70FU   ¼yd (25cm)
Magnolia   GP70MN   ⅝yd (60cm)
Periwinkle   GP70PE   a scrap
Sky   GP70SK   1¼yd (1.15m)
Sprout   GP70SR   ¼yd (25cm)
Turquoise   GP70TQ   ½yd (45cm)
Water   GP70WT   ¼yd (25cm)
ASIAN CIRCLES
Pink   GP89PK   ¾yd (70cm)
PERSIAN VASE
Grey   GP100GY ¾yd (70cm)
Lime   GP100LM ⅜yd (35cm)
MIRAGE STRIPE
Pastel   GP104PT ¼yd (25cm)

SERAPE
Faded   GP111FA 2⅛ yd (1.9m)
ROSETTE
Pink   GP112PK ⅜ yd (35cm)
VARIEGATED IVY
Pink   PJ36PK   ⅝yd (60cm)

BACKING FABRIC 7⅜yd (6.75mm)
We suggest these fabrics for backing
ROSETTE Pink, GP112PK
BABBLE Pink, BM13PK
GUINEA FLOWER Mauve, GP59MV

BINDING
SPOT
Sky   GP70SK   ¾yd (70cm)

BATTING
97in x 97in (246.5cm x 246.5cm).

QUILTING AND EMBROIDERY THREAD
Perle embroidery thread in blue, grey and coral.

OTHER MATERIALS
Freezer paper

TEMPLATES

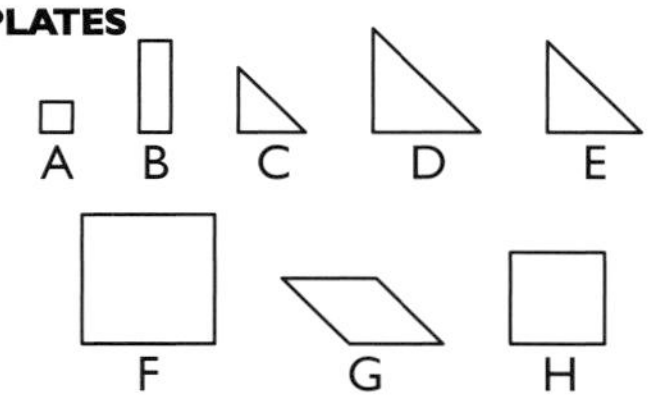

CUTTING OUT
Cut the fabric in the order stated to prevent waste and ensure you have sufficient. Trim and use leftover fabric for later templates as appropriate.

BORDER 1 Cut 2 strips 1½in (3.75cm) wide across the width of the fabric. Cut 2 borders 1½in x 13½in (3.75cm x 34.25cm) for the sides and 2 borders 1½in x 15½in (3.75cm x 39.25cm) for the top and bottom in GP70TQ.

BORDER 3 Cut 4 strips 2in (5cm) wide across the width of the fabric. Cut 2 borders 2in x 25½in (5cm x 64.75cm) for the sides and 2 borders 2in x 28½in (5cm x 72.5cm) for the top and bottom in BM08PT.

BORDER 5 Cut 4 strips 3½in (9cm) wide across the width of the fabric, join as necessary and cut 2 borders 3½in x 36½in (9cm x 92.75cm) for the sides and 2 borders 3½in x 42½in (9cm x 108cm) for the top and bottom in GP111FA.

BORDER 7 Refer to the photograph and fussy cut to match the pattern, 8 strips 2¾in (7cm) wide across the width of the fabric, join as necessary and cut 2 borders 2¾in x 56½in (7cm x 143.5cm) for the sides and 2 borders 2¾in x 61in (7cm x 155cm) for the top and bottom in GP100GY.

BORDER 9 Cut 9 strips 2¾in (7cm) wide across the width of the fabric, join as necessary and cut 2 borders 2¾in x 85in (7cm x 216cm) for the sides and 2 borders 2¾in x 89½in (7cm x 227.25cm) for the top and bottom in GP111FA.

APPLIQUÉ PANEL BACKGROUND Cut 1 square 14in x 14in (35.5cm x 35.5cm) in GP20PT. This is oversize and will be trimmed when the hand appliqué is complete.

APPLIQUÉ SHAPES Please note, the appliqué templates do NOT include a seam allowance.

Cut 1 centre plate and 8 petals in freezer paper, press the shiny side onto the reverse of the fabrics and cut out ¼in (6mm) OUTSIDE the freezer paper, cut 1 centre plate in GP89PK, 4 petals in GP59AP and GP59BL. Leave the freezer paper in place.

TEMPLATE F (Border 6) Cut 5½in (14cm) strips across the width of the fabric. Each strip will give you 7 squares per full width. Cut 7 in BM13PK, GP59AP, GP112PK and PJ36PK. Total 28 squares.

TEMPLATE D (Border 4) Cut 4⅞in (12.5cm) strips across the width of the fabric. Each strip will give you 16 triangles per full width. Note: Cut 2 strips of GP111FA and cut 8 triangles from each row to give variety in the stripes. Cut 9 in GP70SK, 8 in GP70MN, 7 in GP70WT, 6 in GP70SR, 5 in GP70FU, 4 in GP59BL, 2 in GP59MV, GP70PE and 1 in GP60GY. Total 64 triangles.

TEMPLATE E (Border 6) Cut 4³⁄₈in (11cm) strips across the width of the fabric. Each strip will give you 18 triangles per full width. Cut 56 in GP59BL and GP59MV. Total 112 triangles.

TEMPLATE H (Border 8) Cut 4in (10.25cm) strips across the width of the fabric. Each strip will give you 10 squares per full width. Cut 16 in GP89PK, GP70MN, 12 in GP111FA, GP20PT, GP59MV and GP70SK. Total 80 squares.

TEMPLATE C (Borders 2 and 8) Cut 3³⁄₈in (8.5cm) strips across the width of the fabric. Each strip will give you 22 triangles per full width. Cut 64 for border 2 in GP100LM. For border 8 cut 32 in GP89PK, GP70MN, 24 in GP111FA, GP20PT, GP59MV and GP70SK. Total 224 triangles.

TEMPLATE G (Border 8) Cut 3in (7.5cm) strips across the width of the fabric. Each strip will give you 8 diamonds per full width. Cut 32 in GP70TQ, 24 in GP70SK, 16 in GP59AP, GP89PK, 12 in BM13PK, GP70FU, GP104PT, GP111FA, GP112PK and PJ36PK. Total 160 diamonds.

TEMPLATE B (Border 2) Cut 1³⁄₄in (4.5cm) strips across the width of the fabric. Each strip will give you 10 rectangles per full width. Trim to the exact size using the template, cut 32 in GP70SK.

TEMPLATE A (Border 2) Cut 1³⁄₄in (4.5cm) strips across the width of the fabric. Each strip will give you 22 squares per full width. Trim to the exact size using the template, cut 32 in GP70SK and 16 in GP59AP. Total 48 squares.

SASHING (Border 8) Cut 3in (7.5cm) strips across the width of the fabric. Each strip will give you 3 rectangles per full width. Cut 20 rectangles 3in x 12½in (7.5cm x 31.75cm) in BM08PT.

BINDING Cut 10 strips 2½in (6.5cm) across the width of the fabric in GP70SK.

BACKING Cut 2 pieces 40in x 97in (101.5cm x 246.5cm), 2 pieces 40in x 18in (101.5 x 45.75cm) and 1 piece 18in x 18in (45.75cm x 45.75cm) in backing fabric.

MAKING THE APPLIQUÉ PANEL
Use a ¼in seam allowance throughout and refer to quilt assembly diagrams for fabric placement. Working first on the centre plate finger press the seam allowance to the reverse and baste all around, snip the seam allowance as necessary to allow it to lay flat. Carefully position the centre plate in the middle of the background, aligned as shown in appliqué panel diagram a. Appliqué the centre plate into place with invisible stitches, see the Patchwork Know How, Freezer paper section on page 140 for additional information.

Stitch the petals together to form a ring as shown in diagram b and finger press the inner and outer edge seam allowance to the reverse and baste as before. Carefully place the ring on the background as shown in diagram c, there should be an even gap between the centre plate and the ring of petals where the background fabric shows through. Appliqué the ring into place as before. Embroider with chain stitch around the inner and outer edges of the petal ring to give definition using coral perle embroidery thread. Turn the panel to the reverse and cut away the backing behind the appliqué to within ¼in (6mm) of the stitching line. Carefully remove the basting threads and peel off the freezer paper. Trim the panel to 13½in x 13½in (34.25cm x 34.25cm).

BORDERS 1–6
All borders are added to the quilt centre in the same way, sides first, then top and bottom. Refer to the quilt assembly diagrams for fabric placement and piecing order. Add border 1 as shown in quilt assembly diagram 1. Piece 16 blocks for border 2 as shown in block assembly diagrams d and e. The finished border 2 block can be seen in diagram f. Join to form borders and add to the quilt centre as shown.

BLOCK ASSEMBLY DIAGRAMS

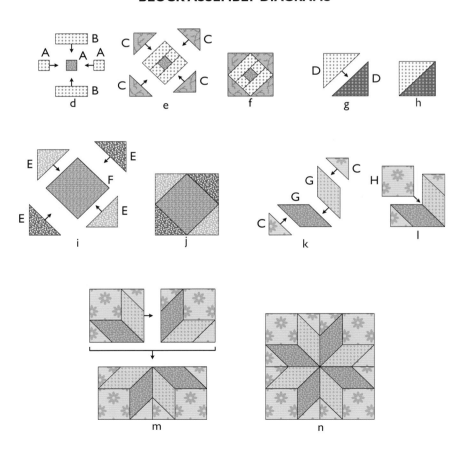

APPLIQUÉ PANEL DIAGRAMS

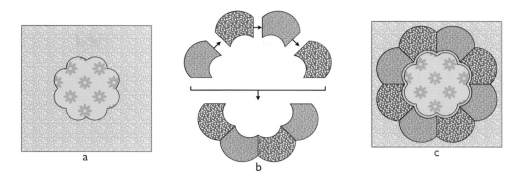

a

b

c

QUILT ASSEMBLY DIAGRAM 1

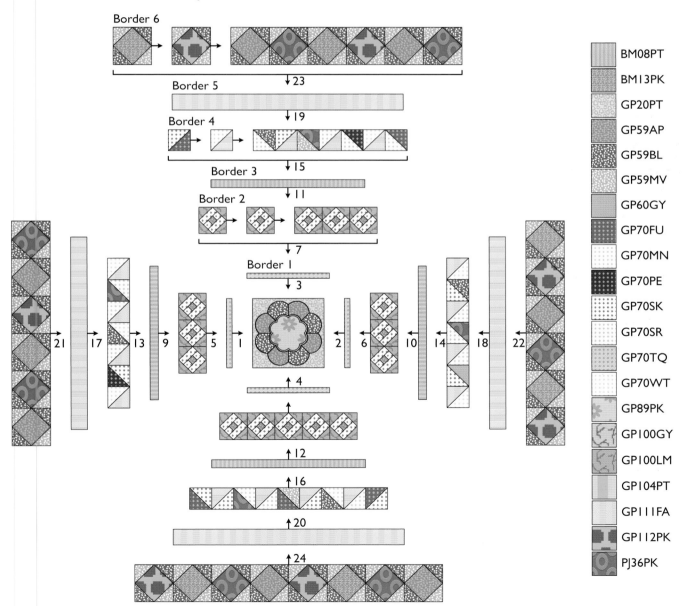

Border 6

↓23

Border 5

↓19

Border 4

↓15

Border 3

↓11

Border 2

↓7

Border 1

↓3

21	17

↑4

↑12

↑16

↑20

↑24

BM08PT

BM13PK

GP20PT

GP59AP

GP59BL

GP59MV

GP60GY

GP70FU

GP70MN

GP70PE

GP70SK

GP70SR

GP70TQ

GP70WT

GP89PK

GP100GY

GP100LM

GP104PT

GP111FA

GP112PK

PJ36PK

Add border 3. Piece 32 blocks for border 4 as shown in diagram g, diagram h shows the finished border 4 block. Join the blocks to form borders and add to the quilt centre. Add border 5. Piece 28 blocks for border 6 as shown in diagram i, the finished border 6 block is shown in diagram j. Join the blocks to form borders and add to the quilt centre.

BORDERS 7 – 9
Add border 7 as shown in quilt assembly diagram 2. Piece 20 blocks for border 8 as shown in block assembly diagrams k, l and m, diagram n shows the finished border 8 block. Join to form borders interspacing with the sashing strips and add to the quilt centre as shown. Finally add border 9 to complete the quilt.

FINISHING THE QUILT
Press the quilt top. Seam the backing pieces using a 1/4in (6mm) seam allowance to form a piece approx. 97in x 97in (246.5cm x 246.5cm). Layer the quilt top, batting and backing and baste together (see page 140). Using perle embroidery thread, quilt in the ditch by hand throughout the quilt. Trim the quilt edges and attach the binding (see page 141).

QUILT ASSEMBLY DIAGRAM 2

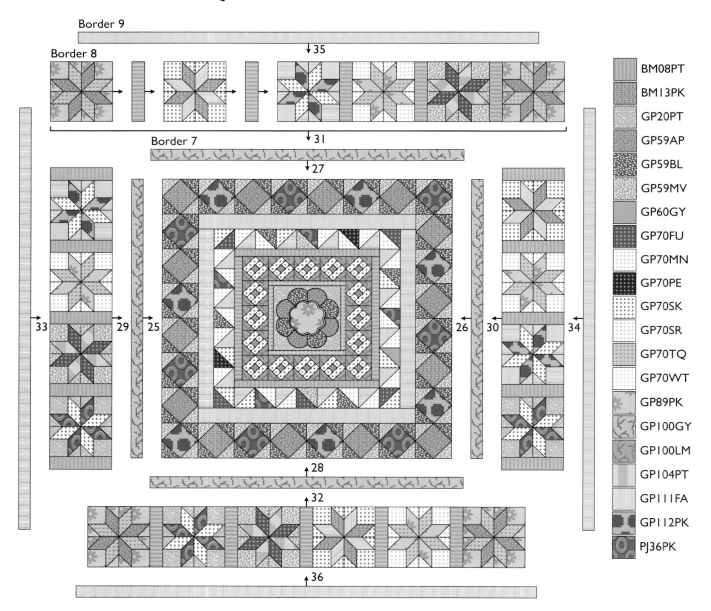

BM08PT
BM13PK
GP20PT
GP59AP
GP59BL
GP59MV
GP60GY
GP70FU
GP70MN
GP70PE
GP70SK
GP70SR
GP70TQ
GP70WT
GP89PK
GP100GY
GP100LM
GP104PT
GP111FA
GP112PK
PJ36PK

vintage ★★
Pauline Smith

2 block types (both finish 4.5in (11.5cm) square) make up this simple alternating design. Hourglass blocks are made using a triangle patch shape (Template K) and nine–patch blocks are made using a square patch shape (Template J). The blocks are straight set into rows to form the quilt centre and surrounded by a simple border. The border fabrics should be cut first and the remaining fabric reserved for template K.

SIZE OF QUILT

The finished quilt will measure approx. 49½in x 58½in (125.5cm x 148.5cm).

MATERIALS

PATCHWORK AND BORDER FABRICS
PAPERWEIGHT
Pastel   GP20PT   ¼yd (25cm)
Sludge   GP20SL   ¾yd (70cm)
GUINEA FLOWER
Mauve   GP59MV   ¼yd (25cm)
SPOT
Apple   GP70AL   ¼yd (25cm)
Chalk   GP70CH   ¼yd (25cm)
China Blue   GP70CI   ¼yd (25cm)
Duck Egg   GP70DE   1⅝yd (1.5m)
incl. Borders
Hydrangea   GP70HY   ⅛ yd (15cm)
Lavender   GP70LV   ⅛ yd (15cm)
MILLEFIORE
Pastel   GP92PT   ¼yd (25cm)
PERSIAN VASE
Grey   GP100GY ¼yd (25cm)
MIRAGE STRIPE
Blue   GP104BL ¼yd (25cm)
COGS
Dusty   GP110DY ¼yd (25cm)
SHOT COTTON
Ecru   SC24   ¼yd (25cm)
Aqua   SC77   ⅛ yd (15cm)

BACKING FABRIC 3⅜yd (3.1m)
We suggest these fabrics for backing
PAPERWEIGHT Pastel, GP20PT
MILLEFIORE Pastel, GP92PT
COGS Dusty, GP110DY

BINDING
MILLEFIORE
Pastel   GP92PT   ½yd (45cm)

BATTING
57in x 66in (145cm x 168cm).

QUILTING THREAD
Toning machine quilting thread and toning perle cotton embroidery thread.

TEMPLATES

CUTTING OUT

Cut the fabric in the order stated to prevent waste.

BORDERS Cut 6 strips 5in (12.75cm) wide across the width of the fabric in GP70DE. Join the strips as necessary and cut 4 borders 5in x 50in (12.75cm x 127cm).

TEMPLATE J Cut 2in (5cm) strips across the width of the fabric. Each strip will give you 20 patches per full width. Cut 53 in GP70CH, 52 in GP104BL, 47 in GP70CI, 45 in GP92PT, GP100GY, 39 in GP110DY, 34 in GP70AL, 32 in GP20PT, 24 in GP59MV, 20 in GP70HY, SC77, 17 in GP70LV and 13 in SC24. Total 441 squares.

TEMPLATE K Cut 5¾in (14.5cm) strips across the width of the fabric. Each strip will give you 24 triangles per full width. Cut 5¾in (14.5cm) squares, cut each square twice diagonally to form 4 triangles using the template as a guide, this will ensure that the long side of the triangle will not have a bias edge. Note: do not move the patches until both the diagonals have been cut. Cut 100 in GP20SL and GP70DE. Total 200 triangles.

BINDING Cut 6 strips 2½in (6.5cm) across the width of the fabric in GP92PT.

BACKING Cut 1 piece 40in x 57in (101.5cm x 145cm) and 1 piece 27in x 57in (68.5cm x 145cm) in backing fabric.

MAKING THE BLOCKS

Use a ¼in (6mm) seam allowance throughout and use the quilt assembly diagram as a guide to fabric placement. Using the template K triangles make a total of 50 hourglass blocks as shown in block assembly diagram a, the finished hourglass block can be seen in diagram b. Using the template J squares make a total of 49 nine–patch blocks as shown in diagram c, the finished nine–patch block can be seen in diagram d.

BLOCK ASSEMBLY DIAGRAMS

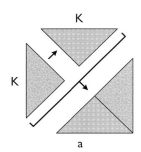

a

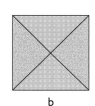

b

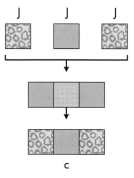

c

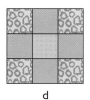

d

MAKING THE QUILT

Lay out the blocks in 11 rows of 9 blocks alternating the hourglass and nine–patch blocks as shown in the quilt assembly diagram. Note that the orientation of the hourglass blocks changes in alternating rows to produce the illusion of larger square blocks set on point. Piece the rows and then join them to form the quilt centre. Add the side borders, then the top and bottom borders to complete the quilt.

FINISHING THE QUILT

Press the quilt top. Seam the backing pieces using a ¼in (6mm) seam allowance to form a piece approx. 57in x 66in (145cm x 168cm). Layer the quilt top, batting and backing and baste together (see page 140). Using toning machine quilting thread quilt in the ditch along the seams between all the blocks and diagonally across the hourglass blocks. Hand quilt in the ditch using toning perle cotton embroidery thread around

the centre square of each nine–patch block. In the border hand quilt, again using the perle cotton embroidery thread, 3 parallel lines offset from the seam by 1in, 2in and 3in (2.5cm, 5cm and 7.5cm). Trim the quilt edges and attach the binding (see page 141).

QUILT ASSEMBLY DIAGRAM

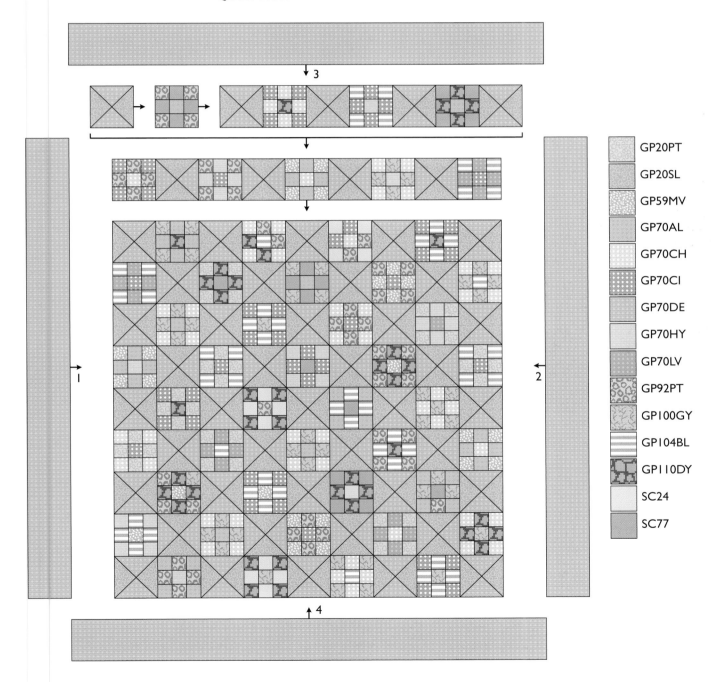

GP20PT
GP20SL
GP59MV
GP70AL
GP70CH
GP70CI
GP70DE
GP70HY
GP70LV
GP92PT
GP100GY
GP104BL
GP110DY
SC24
SC77

honeysuckle afternoons ★★★
Corienne Kramer

The majority of shapes for this quilt are cut to size, we have only provided a template for a small square (Template W) used to make the star points throughout the design. This quilt is made up using large squares of floral print fabrics interspaced with pieced sashing and corner posts, which creates a pattern of Shot Cotton stars at the intersections. The star pattern is continued into the pieced border. Corienne's clever use of Kaffe's new Ombre fabric, which has a graduated colour scale across the width creates lovely halo effects around the stars. A design wall is almost essential for this quilt as careful placing of the sashing and matching of the star points at the intersections are key to the design. We have allowed a little extra Paisley Jungle border fabric, GP60TN, so that some fussy cutting can be done, again the design wall will help with arranging the border patches so that the piecing is not so noticeable.

SIZE OF QUILT
The finished quilt will measure approx.
85in x 97in (216cm x 246.5cm).

MATERIALS
PATCHWORK, SASHING AND
BORDER FABRICS
LOTUS LEAF
Jade   GP29JA   ⅜yd (35cm)
PAISLEY JUNGLE
Lime   GP60LM   ⅜yd (35cm)
Tangerine   GP60TN   1¾yd (1.6m)
ASIAN CIRCLES
Yellow   GP89YE   ⅜yd (35cm)
RADIATION
Yellow   GP115YE   ⅜yd (35cm)
OMBRE
Green   GP117GN   2⅝yd (2.4m)
VARIEGATED LEAVES
Pastel   PJ39PT   ⅜yd (35cm)
Summer   PJ39SU   ⅜yd (35cm)
FRUITFUL
Grey   PJ40GY   ⅜yd (35cm)
JAPANESE CHRYSANTHEMUM
Yellow   PJ41YE   ⅜yd (35cm)
PRIMULA
Cream   PJ42CM   ⅝yd (60cm)
IRIS AND PEONY
Green   PJ43GN   ⅜yd (35cm)
SHOT COTTON
Raspberry   SC08   ⅜yd (35cm)
Lavender   SC14   ⅜yd (35cm)
Watermelon   SC33   ⅜yd (35cm)
Lilac   SC36   ⅜yd (35cm)
Brick   SC58   ⅜yd (35cm)
Granite   SC66   ⅜yd (35cm)
Pudding   SC68   ¼yd (25cm)
Pink   SC83   ⅜yd (35cm)
Blueberry   SC88   ⅜yd (35cm)

BACKING FABRIC 7½yd (6.9m)
We suggest these fabrics for backing
ASIAN CIRCLES Yellow, GP89YE
VARIEGATED LEAVES Pastel, PJ39PT
JAPANESE CHRYSANTHEMUM Yellow,
PJ41YE

BINDING Fabric ⅞yd (80cm)
We suggest these fabrics for binding
SHOT COTTON Raspberry, SC08
or Brick SC58

BATTING
93in x 105in (236cm x 267cm).

QUILTING THREAD
Toning machine quilting thread.

TEMPLATES

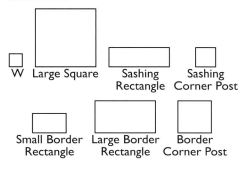

W   Large Square   Sashing   Sashing
                               Rectangle   Corner Post

Small Border   Large Border   Border
Rectangle   Rectangle   Corner Post

CUTTING OUT
LARGE SQUARE Cut 9½in (24.25cm) strips across the width of the fabric. Each strip will give you 4 patches per full width. From these cut 9½in (24.25cm) squares. Cut 6 in PJ42CM, 4 in GP29JA, GP60LM, GP89YE, GP115YE, PJ39PT, PJ39SU, PJ40GY, PJ41YE and PJ43GN. Total 42 squares.

SASHING RECTANGLE Cut 3½in (9cm) strips across the width of the fabric. Each strip will give you 4 patches per full width. Cut 97 strips 3½in x 9½in (9cm x 24.25cm) in GP117GN.

SASHING CORNER POST Cut 3½in (9cm) strips across the width of the fabric. Each strip will give you 11 patches per full width. From these cut 3½in (9cm) squares. Cut 8 in SC14, 7 in SC66, 6 in SC08, SC33, SC36, SC58, SC83, SC88 and 5 in SC68. Total 56 squares.

TEMPLATE W Cut 2in (5cm) strips across the width of the fabric. Each strip will give you 20 patches per full width. Cut 64 in SC14, 56 in SC66, 48 in SC08, SC33, SC36, SC58, SC83, SC88 and 40 in SC68. Total 448 squares.

LARGE BORDER RECTANGLE Cut 5½in (14cm) strips across the width of the fabric. Each strip will give you 4 patches per full width. Cut 26 rectangles 5½in x 9½in (14cm x 24.25cm) in GP60TN. Reserve the remaining fabric for the Border Corner Posts.

BORDER CORNER POST Cut 4 squares 5½in x 5½in (14cm x 14cm) in GP60TN.

SMALL BORDER RECTANGLE Cut 5½in (14cm) strips across the width of the fabric. Each strip will give you 11 patches per full width. Cut 30 rectangles 3½in x 5½in (9cm x 14cm) in GP60TN.

BINDING Cut 10 strips 2½in (6.5cm) across the width of the fabric in binding fabric.

BACKING Cut 2 pieces 40in x 105in (101.5cm x 267cm), 2 pieces 40 in x 14 in (101.5cm x 35.5cm) and 1 piece 26in x 14in (66cm x 35.5cm) in backing fabric.

SASHING & BORDER ASSEMBLY DIAGRAM

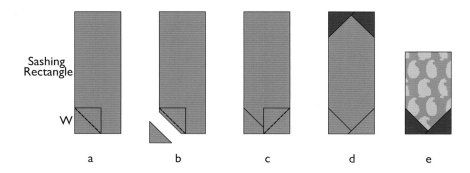

Sashing
Rectangle

W

a   b   c   d   e

MAKING THE QUILT CENTRE

Use a ¼in (6mm) seam allowance throughout and use the quilt assembly diagram as a guide to fabric placement. Using a design wall lay out the Large Squares, Sashing Rectangles and Sashing Corner Posts as shown in the quilt assembly diagram, the Ombre sashing rectangles should be orientated to give the best match at the intersections. Take each sashing rectangle in turn and add the star points as shown in sashing and border assembly diagrams a, b and c. The finished sashing can be seen in diagram d. When each sashing rectangle has its star points

piece the quilt into 15 rows as shown in the quilt assembly diagram. Join the rows to complete the quilt centre.

ADDING THE BORDER

Again using a design wall lay out the GP70TN border patches. Spend a little time arranging the fabric so the pattern is as continuous as possible. Take each small border rectangle in turn and in the same manner as for the sashing add the star points, the finished small border rectangle can be seen in diagram e. Piece the side borders and add to the quilt centre, piece the top and bottom borders and add to the

quilt centre to complete the quilt.

FINISHING THE QUILT

Press the quilt top. Seam the backing pieces using a ¼in (6mm) seam allowance to form a piece approx. 93in x 105in (236cm x 267cm). Layer the quilt top, batting and backing and baste together (see page 140). Using toning machine quilting thread free motion quilt a floral design following the motifs in the large squares. Quilt a floral motif in each star and sashing rectangle. Quilt the border following the paisley design of the fabric. Trim the quilt edges and attach the binding (see page 141).

QUILT ASSEMBLY DIAGRAM

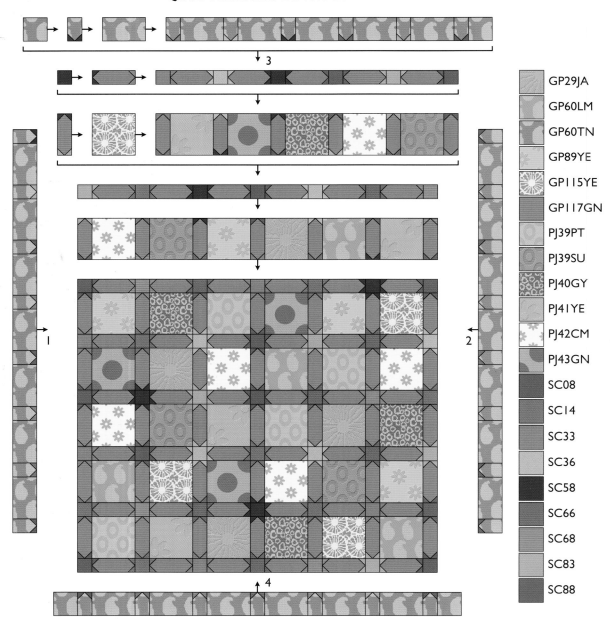

GP29JA
GP60LM
GP60TN
GP89YE
GP115YE
GP117GN
PJ39PT
PJ39SU
PJ40GY
PJ41YE
PJ42CM
PJ43GN
SC08
SC14
SC33
SC36
SC58
SC66
SC68
SC83
SC88

dark windows ★★
Kaffe Fassett

This quilt uses a variation of the classic 'attic windows' block in which the corner square is split into 2 triangles, eliminating the need for fiddly inset seams. The block, which finishes to 9in (22.75cm) is pieced from a triangle patch shape (template R) and a lozenge patch shape (Template S and Reverse S). The blocks are straight set into rows interspaced and surrounded by sashing strips with fussy cut corner posts (both cut to size). The whole quilt centre is the framed with a simple border.

SIZE OF QUILT
The finished quilt will measure approx. 72½in x 72½in (184cm x 184cm).

MATERIALS

PATCHWORK AND SASHING FABRICS
BABBLE		
Ochre	BM13OC	⅜yd (35cm)
PYTHON		
Black	BM16BK	⅜yd (35cm)
Grey	BM16GY	⅜yd (35cm)
ROMAN GLASS		
Gold	GP01GD	⅜yd (35cm)
GUINEA FLOWER		
Brown	GP59BR	⅜yd (35cm)
ASIAN CIRCLES		
Orange	GP89OR	⅜yd (35cm)
MILLEFIORE		
Brown	GP92BR	⅜yd (35cm)
Orange	GP92OR	⅜yd (35cm)
SUZANI		
Black	GP105BK	⅜yd (35cm)
PLINK		
Rust	GP109RU	⅝yd (60cm)
COGS		
Brown	GP110BR	⅜yd (35cm)
PAINTED DAISIES		
Rust	PJ35RU	⅜yd (35cm)
SHOT COTTON		
Thunder	SC06	1⅛yd (1m)
Clementine	SC80	1⅜yd (1.3m)

BORDER FABRIC
WRINKLE		
Brown	BM18BR	2¼yd (2.1m)

BACKING FABRIC 4¾yd (4.3m)
We suggest these fabrics for backing
COGS Brown, GP110BR
PAINTED DAISIES Rust, PJ35RU
MILLEFIORE Brown, GP92BR

BINDING
GUINEA FLOWER		
Brown	GP59BR	⅝yd (60cm)

BATTING
80in x 80in (203cm x 203cm).

QUILTING THREAD
Toning machine quilting thread.

TEMPLATES

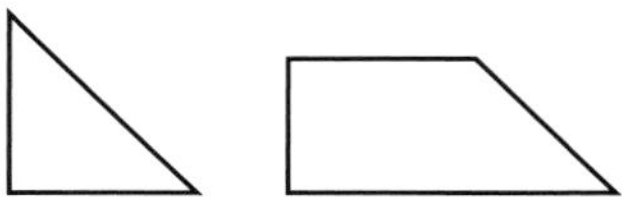

R   S and Reverse S

CUTTING OUT
TEMPLATE R Cut 6in (15.25cm) strips across the width of the fabric. Each strip will give you 12 patches per full width. Cut 72 in SC06.

TEMPLATE S AND REVERSE S Cut 4⅜in (11.25cm) strips across the width of the fabric. Each strip will give you 4 patches per full width. First cut the light fabrics for the top left of each block using the template as drawn. Cut 6 in BM13OC, BM16GY, GP01GD, GP89OR, GP92BR and GP92OR. Flip the template over and the cut the dark fabrics for the bottom right of each block. Cut 6 in BM16BK, GP59BR, GP105BK, GP109RU, GP110BR and PJ35RU.

SASHING STRIPS Cut 2in (5cm) strips across the width of the fabric. Each strip will give you 4 sashing strips per full width. Cut 84 sashing strips 2in x 9½in (5cm x 24.25cm) in SC80.

SASHING CORNER POSTS Fussy cut centring on the floral motifs 49 squares 2in x 2in (5cm x 5cm) in GP109RU.

BORDERS From the length of the fabric cut 2 borders 4½in x 65in (11.5cm x 165cm) for the quilt sides and 2 borders 4½in x 73in (11.5cm x 185.5cm) for the quilt top and bottom in BM18BR.

BINDING Cut 8 strips 2½in (6.5cm) across the width of the fabric in GP59BR.

BACKING Cut 2 pieces 40in x 80in (101.5cm x 203cm) in backing fabric.

MAKING THE QUILT
Use a ¼in (6mm) seam allowance throughout and use the quilt assembly

BLOCK ASSEMBLY DIAGRAM

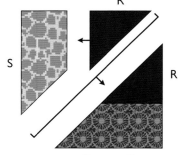

R

S

R

Reverse S

a

b

diagram as a guide to fabric placement. Piece 36 blocks as shown in block assembly diagram a, the finished block can be seen in diagram b. Lay the blocks out as shown in the quilt assembly diagram interspacing with sashing strips and corner posts. Piece the blocks into 13 rows, join the rows to complete the quilt centre.

ADDING THE BORDER

Add the side borders, then the top and bottom borders as indicated in the quilt assembly diagram.

FINISHING THE QUILT

Press the quilt top. Seam the backing pieces using a ¼in (6mm) seam allowance to form a piece approx. 80in x 80in (203cm x 203cm). Layer the quilt top, batting and backing and baste together (see page 140). Quilt in the ditch in all the sashing seams and diagonally across each block in the seam line. Quilt the border with 2 parallel lines offset from the inner seam by 1½in and 3in (3.75cm and 7.5cm). Trim the quilt edges and attach the binding (see page 141).

QUILT ASSEMBLY DIAGRAM

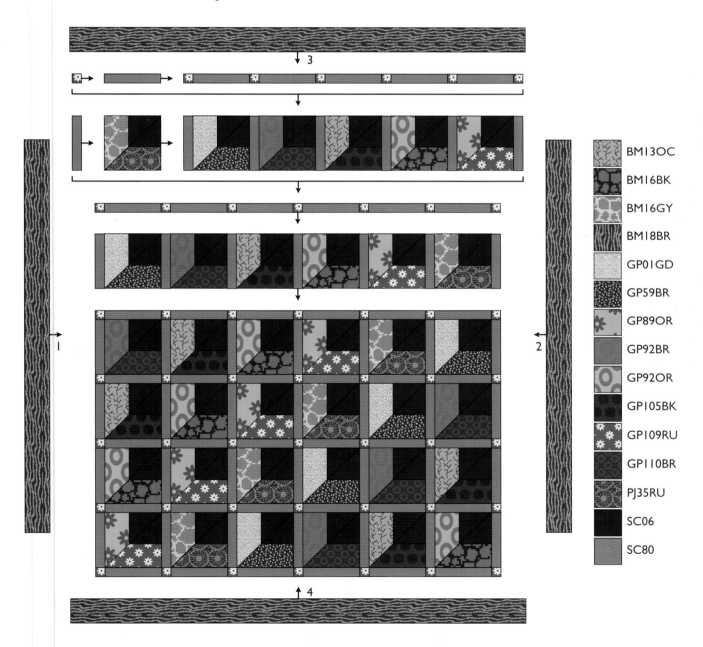

BM13OC
BM16BK
BM16GY
BM18BR
GP01GD
GP59BR
GP89OR
GP92BR
GP92OR
GP105BK
GP109RU
GP110BR
PJ35RU
SC06
SC80

rattan squares ★

Kaffe Fassett

This quilt is made using just 3 patch shapes, Large Square, Small Square and Rectangle, all are cut to size and no templates are provided for these very simple shapes. The quilt is pieced in alternating rows with sashing rectangles interspacing the large squares for one row and sashing rectangles interspacing the small squares which form corner posts for the alternate row.

SIZE OF QUILT
The finished quilt will measure approx. 81½in x 81½in (207cm x 207cm).

MATERIALS

PATCHWORK FABRICS
BABBLE
Ochre   BM13OC   2⅝yds (2.4m)
PYTHON
Grey   BM16GY   ⅜yd (35cm)
ASIAN CIRCLES
Orange   GP89OR   ⅝yd (60cm)
MILLEFIORE
Orange   GP92OR   ⅝yd (60cm)
PERSIAN VASE
Brown   GP100BR ⅜yd (35cm)
ROSETTE
Brown   GP112BR ⅜yd (35cm)
RAMBLING ROSE
Brown   PJ34BR   ⅜yd (35cm)
VARIEGATED IVY
Brown   PJ36BR   ⅜yd (35cm)
SHELL MONTAGE
Beige   PJ37BE   ⅜yd (35cm)
Grey   PJ37GY   ⅜yd (35cm)
POM POM DAHLIAS
Brown   PJ38BR   ⅜yd (35cm)

BACKING FABRIC 5⅞yd (5.4m)
We suggest these fabrics for backing
SUZANI Black, GP105BK
ASIAN CIRCLES Orange, GP89OR
PYTHON Grey, BM16GY

BINDING
BUTTONS
Ochre   GP101OC   ¾yd (70cm)

BATTING
89in x 89in (226cm x 226cm).

QUILTING THREAD
Toning machine quilting thread.

TEMPLATES

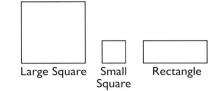

Large Square   Small   Rectangle
                Square

CUTTING OUT
Large Square Cut 10in (25.5cm) strips across the width of the fabric. Each strip will give you 4 patches per full width. Cut 5 in GP89OR, 4 in BM16GY, GP100BR, GP112BR, PJ34BR, PJ36BR, PJ37BE, PJ37GY and 3 in PJ38BR. Total 36 squares.

SMALL SQUARE Cut 4in (10.25cm) strips across the width of the fabric. Each strip will give you 10 patches per full width. Cut 49 squares 4in x 4in (10.25cm x 10.25cm) in GP92OR.

RECTANGLE Cut 4in (10.25cm) strips across the width of the fabric. Each strip will give you 4 patches per full width. Cut 84 rectangles 4in x 10in (10.25cm x 25.5cm) in BM13OC.

BINDING Cut 9 strips 2½in (6.5cm) across the width of the fabric in GP101OC.

BACKING Cut 2 pieces 40in x 89in (101.5cm x 226cm), 2 pieces 40in x 10in (101.5cm x 25.5cm) and 1 piece 10in x 10in (25.5cm x 25.5cm) in backing fabric. For a quirky look to the backing you could cut the 10in (25.5cm) square from a different fabric and piece the backing with the contrasting square in the centre.

MAKING THE QUILT
Use a ¼in (6mm) seam allowance throughout and use the quilt assembly diagram as a guide to fabric placement. Piece 13 rows as shown in the quilt assembly diagram then join them to complete the quilt.

FINISHING THE QUILT
Press the quilt top. Seam the backing pieces using a ¼in (6mm) seam allowance to form a piece approx. 89in x 89in (226cm x 226cm). Layer the quilt top, batting and backing and baste together (see page 140). Using toning machine quilting thread quilt in the ditch along all the seams, then quilt additional lines across the large squares offset from the edges by 3in (7.5cm) as shown in the quilting diagram. Trim the quilt edges and attach the binding (see page 141).

QUILTING DIAGRAM

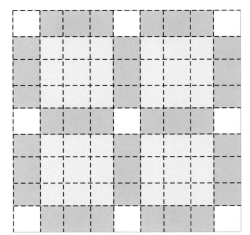

QUILT ASSEMBLY DIAGRAM

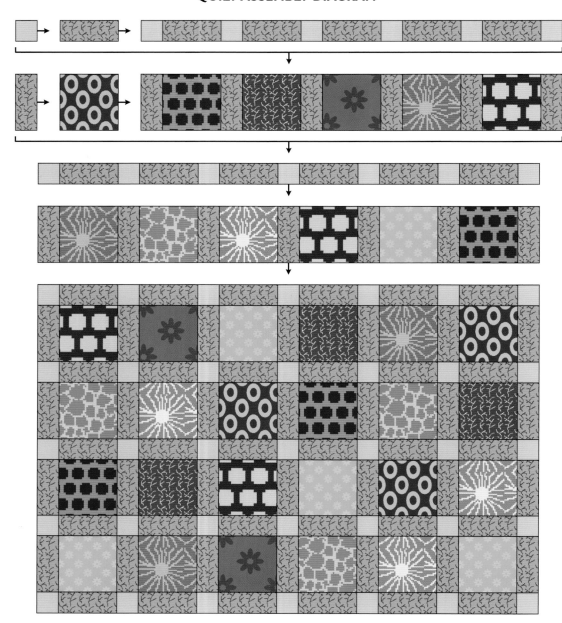

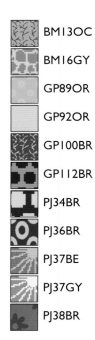

BM13OC

BM16GY

GP89OR

GP92OR

GP100BR

GP112BR

PJ34BR

PJ36BR

PJ37BE

PJ37GY

PJ38BR

sunlight in the forest ★★
Kaffe Fassett

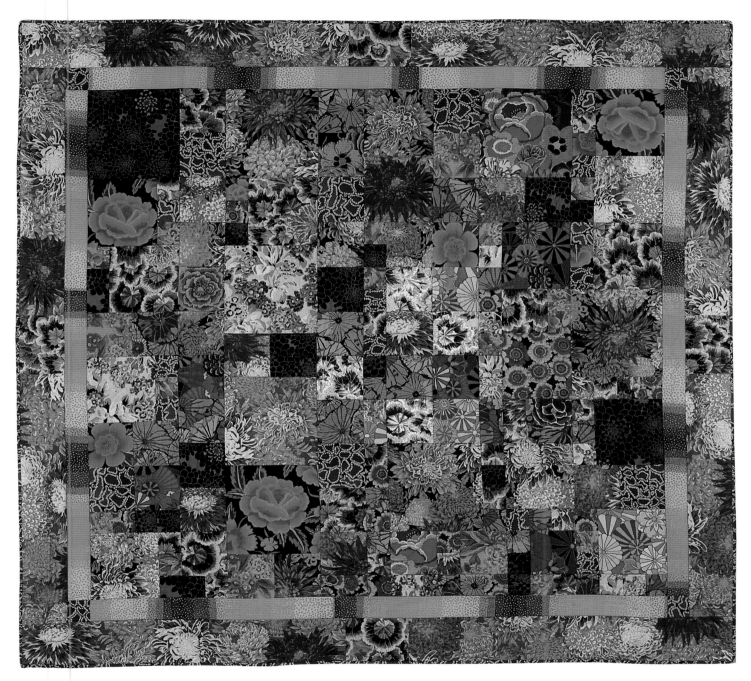

This centre of this quilt is made using 4 sizes of square, Very Large, Large, Medium and Small square, all are cut to size and no templates are provided for these very simple shapes. We have allowed extra fabric for fussy cutting the blooms in the Embroidered Shawl, Bekah and Japanese Chrysanthemum fabrics which are crucial to the design. The quilt is pieced into sections and columns which are joined to form the quilt centre. The centre is then surrounded with a simple inner border with corner posts and an outer border pieced of sections cut to size.

SIZE OF QUILT
The finished quilt will measure approx. 93in x 87in (236cm x 221cm).

MATERIALS
PATCHWORK AND BORDER FABRICS
Extra fabric has been included for fussy cutting as detailed above.

PYTHON
Black   BM16BK   ½yd (45cm)
LOTUS LEAF
Umber   GP29UM   ⅝yd (60cm)
BEKAH
Plum   GP69PL   ½yd (45cm)
EMBROIDERED SHAWL
Red   GP106RD ¾yd (70cm)
RADIATION
Black   GP115BK ⅜yd (35cm)
Brown   GP115BR ⅜yd (35cm)
LINE DANCE
Black   GP116BK ⅝yd (60cm)
OMBRE
Green   GP117GN ⅞yd (80cm)
PAINTED DAISIES
Rust   PJ35RU   ⅜yd (35cm)
VARIEGATED LEAVES
Brown   PJ39BR   ⅞yd (80cm)
Mauve   PJ39MV   ¼yd (25cm)
JAPANESE CHRYSANTHEMUM
Brown   PJ41BR   2¼yd (2.1m)
Red   PJ41RD   1⅛yd (1m)
PRIMULA
Magenta   PJ42MG   ⅜yd (35cm)
Taupe   PJ42TA   ¾yd (70cm)

BACKING FABRIC 7⅝yd (7m)
We suggest these fabrics for backing
BEKAH Plum, GP69PL
VARIEGATED LEAVES Mauve, GP39BR
EMBROIDERED SHAWL Red, GP106RD

BINDING
PYTHON
Black   BM16BK   ⅞yd (80cm)

BATTING
101in x 95in (256.5cm x 241.5cm).

QUILTING THREAD
Toning hand quilting thread.

TEMPLATES

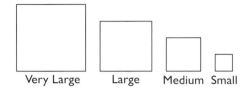

Very Large   Large   Medium Small

CUTTING OUT
Our usual method of cutting strips the full width of the fabric would be very wasteful in this case and we have not allowed enough fabric for this technique. To reduce waste we suggest drawing out the required shapes onto the reverse of the fabrics for the best fit before cutting. For fabrics GP106RD, GP69PL and PJ41RD centre the squares on the most prominent blooms in the fabric design, refer to the photograph for help with this.

OUTER BORDER Cut 4 strips 6½in x 40in (16.5cm x 101.5cm) in PJ41BR and 2 strips 6½in x 14½in (16.5cm x 36.75cm) in PJ39BR for the quilt top and bottom. Cut 4 strips 6½in x 34in (16.5cm x 86.25cm) in PJ41BR and 2 strips 6½in x 8½in (16.5cm x 21.5cm) in PJ39BR for the quilt sides.

VERY LARGE SQUARE Cut 12½in (31.75cm) squares. Cut 3 in PJ41RD, 1 in GP69PL, GP116BK, PJ41BR, PJ42TA and GP106RD. Total 8 squares.

LARGE SQUARE Cut 9½in (24.25cm) Squares. Cut 3 in PJ39BR, PJ41RD, 2 in GP106RD, PJ41BR, 1 in GP115BK, GP115BR, GP116BK, PJ35RU and PJ42TA. Total 15 squares.

MEDIUM SQUARE Cut 6½in (16.5cm) squares. Cut 8 in GP28UM, 7 in PJ41RD, 6 in BM16BK, 5 in PJ41BR, 4 in GP69PL, GP115BK, GP116BK, PJ39BR, PJ39MV, PJ42MG, 2 in GP115BR and GP106RD. Total 54 squares.

SMALL SQUARES Cut 3½in (9cm) squares. Cut 15 in BM16BK (includes 4 squares for

BORDER ASSEMBLY DIAGRAM

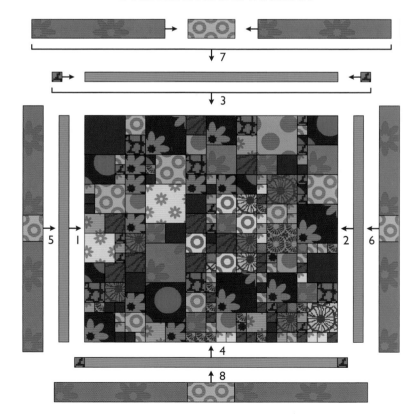

inner border corner posts), 14 in GP29UM, PJ39BR, PJ42MG, 13 in GP116BK, 12 in PJ35RU, 8 in PJ42TA, 4 in PJ41BR, 3 in GP106RD, 2 in PJ41RD and 1 in GP115BR. Total 100 squares.

INNER BORDER Cut 8 strips 3½in (9cm) wide across the width of the fabric, join as necessary and cut 2 borders 3½in x 75½in (9cm x 191.75cm) for the quilt top and bottom and 2 borders 3½in x 69½in (9cm x 176.5cm) for the quilt sides in GP117GN.

BINDING Cut 10 strips 2½in (6.5cm) across the width of the fabric in BM16BK.

BACKING Cut 2 pieces 40in x 95in (101.5cm x 241.25cm), 2 pieces 40in x 22in (101.5cm x 56cm) and 1 piece 22in x 22in (56cm x 56cm) in backing fabric. For a quirky look to the backing you could cut

the 22in (56cm) square from a different fabric and piece the backing with the contrasting square in the centre.

MAKING THE QUILT
Use a ¼in (6mm) seam allowance throughout and use the quilt assembly diagram as a guide to fabric placement. Piece the quilt in sections and columns as shown. Work from right to left for this quilt, the first column will set the method and allow you to work out the piecing order for all the following sections and columns. Join the columns to form the quilt centre.

ADDING THE BORDERS
Add the side inner borders to the quilt centre, then add a corner post to each end of the top and bottom inner borders and add to the quilt centre. Piece the side outer

borders as shown in the border assembly diagram and add to the quilt centre. Piece the top and bottom borders in the same way and add to the quilt centre to complete the quilt.

FINISHING THE QUILT
Press the quilt top. Seam the backing pieces using a ¼in (6mm) seam allowance to form a piece approx. 101in x 95in (256.5cm x 241.5cm). Layer the quilt top, batting and backing and baste together (see page 140). Using toning hand quilting thread quilt the very large and large squares diagonally in both directions and the medium and small squares diagonally in one direction alternating the directions to form zigzags wherever possible. In the outer border quilt a line offset from the inner seam by approx. 2in (5cm). Trim the quilt edges and attach the binding (see page 141).

QUILT ASSEMBLY DIAGRAM

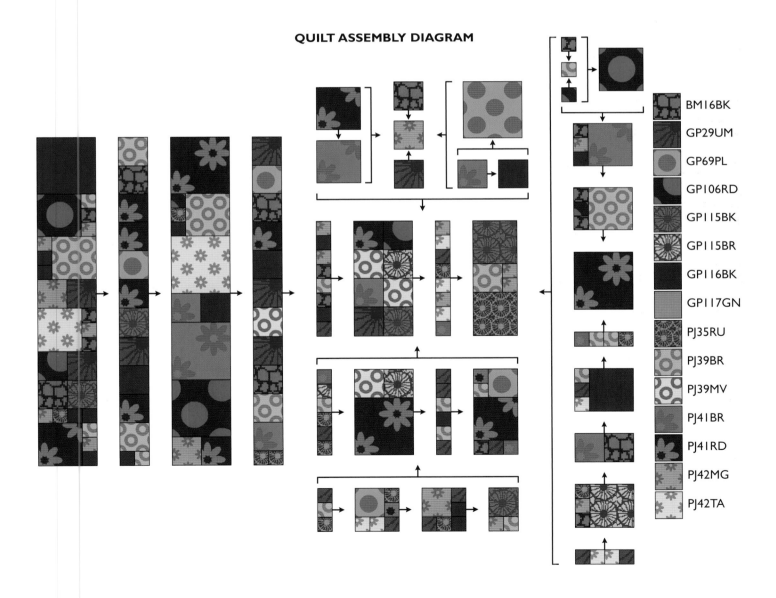

BM16BK
GP29UM
GP69PL
GP106RD
GP115BK
GP115BR
GP116BK
GP117GN
PJ35RU
PJ39BR
PJ39MV
PJ41BR
PJ41RD
PJ42MG
PJ42TA

parquet ★★
Kaffe Fassett

This quilt is pieced in columns, starting at the bottom with a triangle patch shape (Template JJ). 2 lozenge patch shapes (Templates LL and MM) are added alternately, to make a column with 2 further lozenge shapes (Templates KK and NN) used only at the top and bottom of each column. The columns are then joined and the top edge is filled using more template JJ triangles and a further triangle patch shape (Template OO). The fabrics are distributed in a structured way alternating across the quilt and the stripe directions are important to the overall design. The quilt centre is surrounded with a simple border to frame the quilt.

SIZE OF QUILT
The finished quilt will measure approx.
71in x 82½in (180cm x 209cm).

MATERIALS
PATCHWORK AND BORDER FABRICS
STRAWS
Rust   BM08RU ⅝yd (60cm)
SHELLSCAPE
Rust   BM14RU ½yd (45cm)
PYTHON
Brown   BM16BR ⅜yd (35cm)
ABORIGINAL DOTS
Purple   GP71PU ⅜yd (35cm)
ASIAN CIRCLES
Orange   GP89OR ¾yd (70cm)
MILLEFIORE
Brown   GP92BR 1½yd (1.4m)
Orange   GP92OR ½yd (45cm)
PERSIAN VASE
Brown   GP100BR ⅜yd (35cm)
MIRAGE STRIPE
Brown   GP104BR ¾yd (70cm)
PLINK
Rust   GP109RU ⅜yd (35cm)
COGS
Dusty   GP110DY ½yd (45cm)
ROSETTE
Brown   GP112BR ½yd (45cm)
RAMBLING ROSE
Brown   PJ34BR ⅜yd (35cm)
VARIEGATED IVY
Lavender   PJ36LV ⅜yd (35cm)
SHELL MONTAGE
Grey   PJ37GY ½yd (45cm)
VARIEGATED LEAVES
Brown   PJ39BR ⅜yd (35cm)

BACKING FABRIC 5⅜yd (4.9m)
We suggest these fabrics for backing
PLINK Rust, GP109RU
ASIAN CIRCLES Orange, GP89OR
SHELL MONTAGE Grey, PJ37GY.

BINDING
MIRAGE STRIPE
Brown   GP104BR ⅝yd (60cm)

BATTING
79in x 90in (200.5cm x 228.5cm).

QUILTING THREAD
Toning machine quilting threads.

TEMPLATES

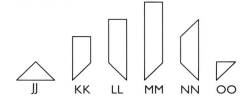

JJ   KK   LL   MM   NN   OO

CUTTING OUT
Cut the fabrics in the order stated, use leftover strips for subsequent templates wherever possible. The stripe fabrics, BM08RU and GP104BR are cut down the length so that the stripes run down the length of the lozenge patches, all other fabrics are cut across the width in the normal manner.

TEMPLATE JJ Cut a 6½in (16.5cm) strip across the width of the fabric. Align the long edge of the triangle with the stripes and cut 9 triangles in BM08RU. Refer to the quilt assembly diagram for help with this. Reserve the remaining strip for template OO.

TEMPLATE OO Using the remaining strip from template JJ, cut 2 triangles in BM08RU. Check that the stripe direction will run correctly when the patches are stitched.

BORDERS Cut 8 strips 5in (12.75cm) wide across the width of the fabric, join as necessary and cut 2 borders 5in x 75in (12.75cm x 190.5cm) for the quilt top and bottom and 2 borders 5in x 72½in (12.75cm x 184.25cm) for the quilt sides in GP92BR. These are a little oversized and will be trimmed to fit exactly later.

TEMPLATE MM Fabrics BM08RU and GP104BR cut a 12in (30.5cm) strip across the width of the fabric. With the long side of the template aligned with the stripes cut 10 in GP104BR and 5 in BM08RU. For all other fabrics cut 3in (7.5cm) strips across the width of the fabric. Each strip will give you 3 patches per full width. Cut 8 in GP89OR, GP110DY, GP112BR, 7 in BM14RU, PJ37GY, 5 in BM16BR, GP71PU, GP92BR, GP100BR, GP109RU, PJ34BR, PJ36LV, PJ39BR and 2 in GP92OR. Total 95 patches.

TEMPLATE LL Fabrics BM08RU and GP104BR cut a 9½in (24.25cm) strip across the width of the fabric. With the long side of the template aligned with the stripes cut 10 in GP104BR and 5 in BM08RU. For all other fabrics cut 3in (7.5cm) strips across the width of the fabric. Each strip will give you 4 patches per full width. Cut 11 in GP89OR, 8 in GP110DY, GP112BR, 7 in BM14RU, PJ37GY, 5 in BM16BR, GP71PU, GP92BR, GP100BR, GP109RU, PJ34BR, PJ36LV, PJ39BR and 4 in GP92OR. Total 100 patches.

COLUMN ASSEMBLY DIAGRAM

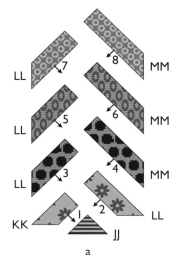

a   b

TEMPLATE NN Cut 3in (7.5cm) strips across the width of the fabric. Each strip will give you 5 patches per full width. Cut 6 in GP92OR and 4 in GP89OR. Total 10 patches.

TEMPLATE KK Cut 3in (7.5cm) strips across the width of the fabric. Cut 3 in GP89OR and 2 in GP92OR. Total 5 patches.

BINDING Cut 8 strips 2½in (6.5cm) wide across the width of the fabric in GP104BR.

BACKING Cut 2 pieces 40in x 90in (101.5cm x 228.5) in backing fabric.

MAKING THE QUILT

Use a ¼in (6mm) seam allowance throughout and use the quilt assembly diagram as a guide to fabric placement. Piece each column from the bottom, starting with a template JJ triangle. Follow column assembly diagrams a and b, first adding template KK and template LL lozenges. The column is then built by adding template LL and MM lozenges alternately. When the column is almost complete add the template NN lozenges as shown in the quilt assembly diagram. Make 5 columns and join carefully, the edges will be a bit stretchy as they are bias cut. Fill in the top edge with template JJ triangles, using the inset seam method as shown in the Patchwork Knowhow section at the back of the book. Finally add the template OO triangles to the top corners to complete the quilt centre.

ADDING THE BORDER

Add the side borders and trim to fit exactly, finally add the top and bottom borders and trim to complete the quilt.

FINISHING THE QUILT

Press the quilt top. Seam the backing pieces using a ¼in (6mm) seam allowance to form a piece approx. 79in x 90in (200.5cm x 228.5cm). Layer the quilt top, batting and backing and baste together (see page 140). Stitch in the ditch throughout the quilt using toning machine quilting thread. Trim the quilt edges and attach the binding (see page 141).

QUILT ASSEMBLY DIAGRAM

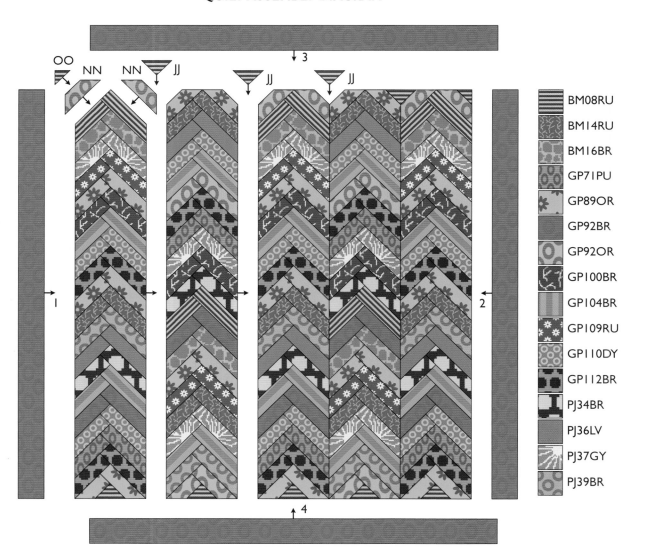

BM08RU
BM14RU
BM16BR
GP71PU
GP89OR
GP92BR
GP92OR
GP100BR
GP104BR
GP109RU
GP110DY
GP112BR
PJ34BR
PJ36LV
PJ37GY
PJ39BR

shells ★★
Liza Prior Lucy

This quilt is pieced in stages. First small 9–patch blocks are pieced using a small square patch shape (Template J), these are made from the dark and light fabrics, each using 5 dark and 4 light squares alternated. The exact combination of fabrics is not important, mix it up! The small 9–patch blocks are then combined with medium squares (Template M) to make 'double' 9–patch blocks. These are then set on point diagonally, alternating with large squares of feature Shell Montage fabric (cut to size), the row ends and quilt corners are filled with side and corner setting triangles (cut to size). The completed quilt centre is finally framed with a simple border.

SIZE OF QUILT
The finished quilt will measure approx. 85½in x 85½in (217cm x 217cm).

MATERIALS
PATCHWORK FABRICS
PAPERWEIGHT
Paprika	GP20PP	1yd (90cm)
Sludge	GP20SL	¾yd (70cm)

SHELL MONTAGE
Beige	PJ37BE	3⅛ yd (2.9m)

LIGHT FABRICS FOR SMALL 9–PATCH BLOCKS
Buy ¼yd (25cm) of each
ABORIGINAL DOTS
Gold	GP71GD
Ochre	GP71OC

SHOT COTTON
Sprout	SC94
Honeydew	SC95

DARK FABRICS FOR SMALL 9–PATCH BLOCKS
Buy ¼yd (25cm) of each
ABORIGINAL DOTS
Forest	GP71FO
Ocean	GP71ON

SHOT COTTON
Pewter	SC22
Bronze	SC69
Steel	SC75

BORDER FABRIC
PLINK
Rust	GP109RU	2⅝yd (2.4m)

BACKING FABRIC 6¾yd (6.2m)
We suggest these fabrics for backing
MILLEFIORE Brown, GP92BR
SHELL MONTAGE Beige, PJ37BE

BINDING
DIAGONAL STRIPE
Ochre	GP90OC	⅞yd (80cm)

BATTING
93in x 93in (236cm x 236cm).

QUILTING THREAD
Khaki machine quilting thread.

TEMPLATES
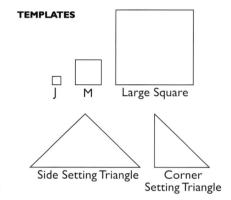
J M Large Square

Side Setting Triangle Corner Setting Triangle

CUTTING OUT
We have included a cutting layout for fabric PJ37BE and we suggest drawing out the large shapes to get the best fit before cutting this fabric.

BORDERS From the length of the fabric cut 2 borders 5in x 78in (12.75cm x 198cm) for the quilt sides and 2 borders 5in x 87in (12.75cm x 221cm) for the quilt top and bottom in GP109RU. These are a little oversized and will be trimmed to fit exactly later.

SIDE SETTING TRIANGLE Cut 3 squares 20⅜in x 20⅜in (51.75cm x 51.75cm) in PJ37BE, cut each square twice diagonally to make 4 triangles, this will ensure that the long side of the triangles will not have a bias edge. Note: Do not move the squares until both diagonals have been cut. Total 12 triangles.

LARGE SQUARE Cut 9 squares 14in x 14in (35.5cm x 35.5cm) in PJ37BE.

CORNER SETTING TRIANGLE Cut 2 squares 10⅜in x 10⅜in (26.5cm x 26.5cm) in PJ37BE, cut each square diagonally to form 2 triangles. Total 4 triangles.

TEMPLATE J Cut 2in (5cm) strips across the width of the fabric. Each strip will give you 20 patches per full width. Cut 320 in Dark fabrics and 256 in Light fabrics. Total 576 squares.

TEMPLATE M Cut 5in (12.75cm) strips across the width of the fabric. Each strip will give you 8 patches per full width. Cut 48 in GP20PP and 32 in GP20SL. Total 80 squares.

CUTTING LAYOUT FOR FABRIC PJ37BE

BLOCK ASSEMBLY DIAGRAM
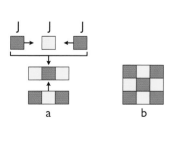
a

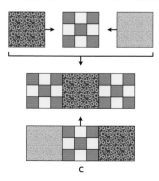
b

c

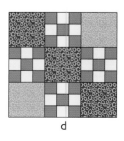
d

BINDING Cut 9¾yd (8.9m) of 2½in (6.5cm) wide bias binding in GP90OC.

BACKING Cut 2 pieces 40in x 93in (101.5cm x 236cm), 2 pieces 40in x 14in (101.5cm x 35.5cm) and 1 piece 14in x 14in (35.5cm x 35.5cm) in backing fabric. For a quirky look to the backing you could cut the 14in (35.5cm) square from a different fabric and piece the backing with the contrasting square in the centre.

MAKING THE BLOCKS

Use a ¼in (6mm) seam allowance throughout and use the quilt assembly diagram as a guide to fabric placement. Make a total of 64 small 9–patch blocks as shown in block assembly diagram a, each block should have 5 dark and 4 light squares alternated. The exact combination of fabrics is not important. The finished small 9–patch block can be seen in diagram b. Next make 16 'double' 9–patch blocks as shown in diagram c. Each takes 4 small 9–patch blocks and 5 template M squares, 3 in GP20PP and 2 in GP20SL. The position of the colours is important. The finished double 9–patch block can be seen in diagram d.

MAKING THE QUILT CENTRE

Lay the 'double' 9–patch blocks out on point as shown in the quilt assembly diagram, with the strong pink GP20PP squares running in vertical rows. Alternate the pieced blocks with the large squares. Add the side setting triangles and corner setting triangles to complete the edges and corners of the centre. Carefully separate into diagonal rows and join. Join the rows to complete the quilt centre.

ADDING THE BORDER

Trim the side borders to fit exactly and join to the quilt centre. Trim the top and bottom borders to fit exactly then join to the quilt centre as shown in the quilt assembly diagram.

FINISHING THE QUILT

Press the quilt top. Seam the backing pieces using a ¼in (6mm) seam allowance to form a piece approx. 93in x 93in (236cm x 236cm). Layer the quilt top, batting and backing and baste together (see page 140). Using khaki machine quilting thread meander quilt around the large shell shapes to make them appear embossed and meander all over the pieced blocks. Trim the quilt edges and attach the binding (see page 141).

QUILT ASSEMBLY DIAGRAM

- GP20PP
- GP20SL
- GP109RU
- PJ37BE
- Lights
- Darks

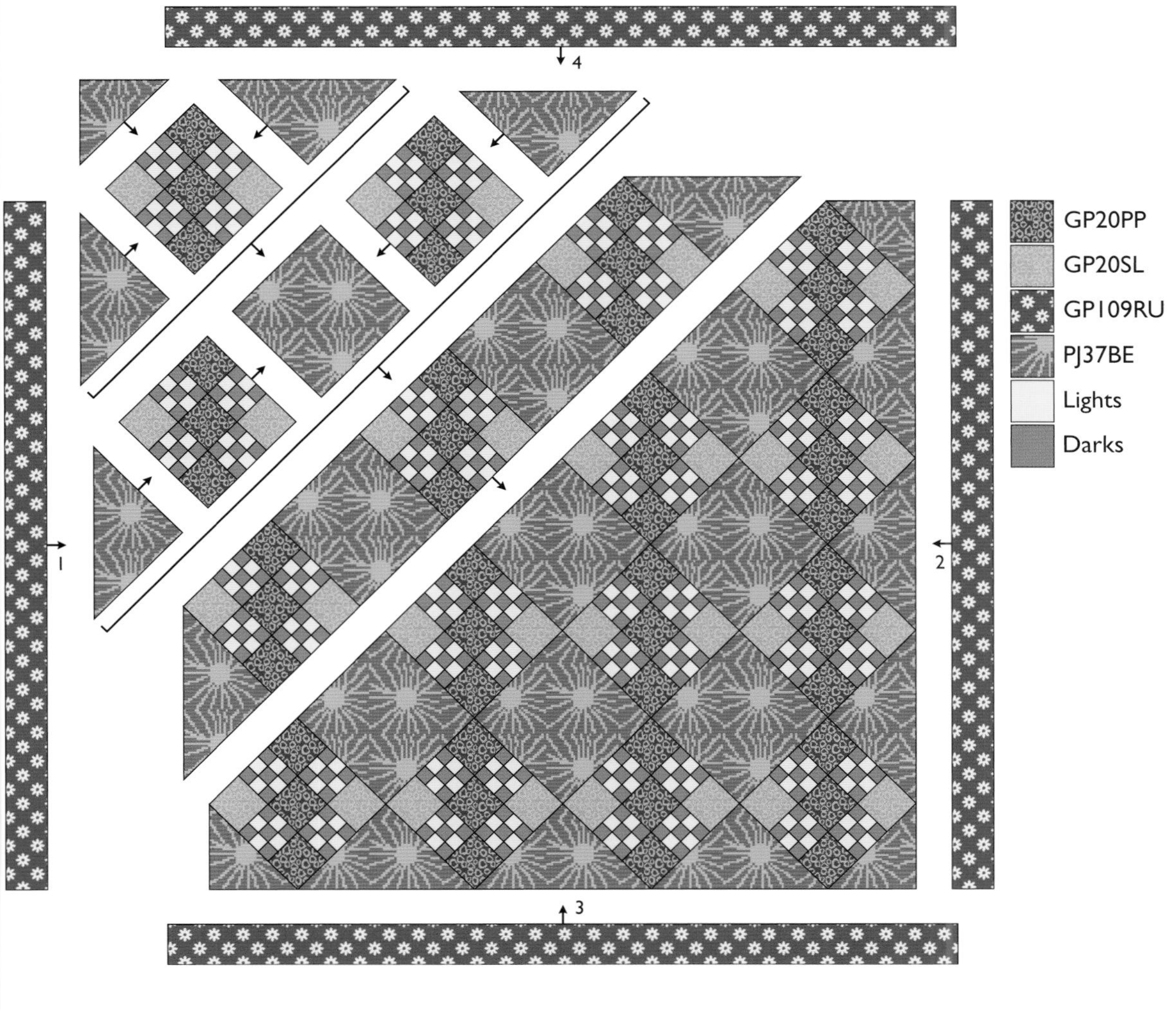

dark kites ★★★
Kaffe Fassett

The large blocks in the centre and small blocks in the border of this quilt are each pieced from '4–triangle' units. These are made using 2 squares of fabric (cut to size) which are sewn, cut, then sewn and cut again to yield 2 '4–triangle' units. Full instructions on how to piece the '4–triangle' units are given below. The large '4–triangle' units, which finish to 7in (17.75cm), are pieced into blocks for the quilt centre. The blocks are set on point diagonally, alternating with setting squares (cut to size), the row ends and quilt corners are filled with side and corner setting triangles (cut to size). The completed quilt centre is framed with a border pieced using small '4–triangle' units, which finish to 3½in (9cm), along with 2 triangle patch shapes (Templates Y and C). Spacer rectangles (trimmed to fit) are used to bring the pieced borders to the correct length before pieced corner posts are added to complete the quilt.

SIZE OF QUILT
The finished quilt will measure approx. 70in x 90in (178cm x 228.5cm).

MATERIALS
PATCHWORK AND BORDER FABRICS
BABBLE
Charcoal   BM13CC 2½yd (2.3m)
SHELLSCAPE
Charcoal   BM14CC 1⅜yd (1.3m)
Red   BM14RD ½yd (45cm)
RINGS
Black   BM15BK ¼yd (25cm)
PYTHON
Black   BM16BK ¼yd (25cm)
Blue   BM16BL ½yd (45cm)
Brown   BM16BR ¼yd (25cm)
ROMAN GLASS
Byzantine   GP01BY ¼yd (25cm)
GUINEA FLOWER
Brown   GP59BR ¼yd (25cm)
SPOT
Burgundy   GP70BG ½yd (45cm)
Sapphire   GP70SP ¼yd (25cm)
ABORIGINAL DOTS
Chocolate   GP71CL ¼yd (25cm)
MILLEFIORE
Blue   GP92BL ¼yd (25cm)
PLINK
Black   GP109BK ¼yd (25cm)
COGS
Brown   GP110BR ¼yd (25cm)
Green   GP110GN ¼yd (25cm)
ROSETTE
Dark   GP112DK ½yd (45cm)
SHOT COTTON
Thunder   SC06   ½yd (45cm)
Bordeaux   SC54   ½yd (45cm)
Eucalyptus   SC90   ¼yd (25cm)

BACKING FABRIC 5¾yd (5.3m)
We suggest these fabrics for backing
PLINK Black, GP109BK
PYTHON Black, BM16BK
SPOT Burgundy, GP70BG

BINDING
SPOT
Black   GP70BK ¾yd (70cm)

BATTING
78in x 98in (198cm x 249cm).

QUILTING THREAD
Toning machine quilting thread.

TEMPLATES

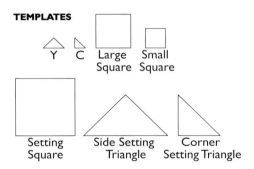

Y   C   Large   Small
        Square Square

Setting   Side Setting   Corner
Square   Triangle   Setting Triangle

CUTTING OUT
We have included a cutting layout for fabric BM13CC and we suggest drawing out the large shapes to get the best fit before cutting this fabric.

SIDE SETTING TRIANGLE Cut 2 squares 21⅛in x 21⅛in (53.75cm x 53.75cm) in BM13CC, cut each square twice diagonally to make 4 triangles, this will ensure that the long side of the triangles will not have a bias edge. Note: Do not move the squares until both diagonals have been cut. This will make 8 triangles. Using one of the triangles as a template, align the long side with the straight grain and cut an additional 2 triangles. Total 10 triangles.

SETTING SQUARE Cut 6 squares 14½in x 14½in (37cm x 37cm) in BM13CC

CORNER SETTING TRIANGLE Cut 2 squares 10⅞in x 10⅞in (27.75cm x 27.75cm) in BM13CC, cut each square diagonally to form 2 triangles. Total 4 triangles.

LARGE SQUARES Cut 8¼in (21cm) wide strips across the width of the fabric. From

the strips cut 8¼in (21cm) squares, each strip will give you 4 squares per full width. Cut 6 in SC06, 4 in GP71CL, 3 in BM14RD, BM14CC, BM16BL, GP110BR, GP112DK, SC54, 2 in BM16BK, BM16BR, GP01BY, GP59BR, GP70BG, GP70SP, GP92BL, GP110GN, SC90, 1 in BM15BK and GP109BK. Total 48 squares. Trim any remaining strips and use for Small Squares.

SMALL SQUARES Cut 4¾in (12cm) wide strips across the width of the fabric From the strips cut 4¾in (12cm) squares, each strip will give you 8 squares per full width. Cut 8 in SC54, 6 in GP70BG, 5 in BM14RD, GP70SP, SC90, 4 in BM16BL, GP92BL, GP109BK, GP112DK, 3 in BM16BK, GP59BR, GP110GN, 2 in GP110BR, 1 in BM16BR and GP01BY. Total 58 Squares.

TEMPLATE Y Cut 6¼in (16cm) strips across the width of the fabric. Each strip will give you 24 triangles per full width. Cut 6¼in (16cm) squares, cut each square twice diagonally to form 4 triangles using the template as a guide, this will ensure that the long side of the triangle will not have a bias edge. Note: do not move the patches until both the diagonals have been cut. Cut 96 in BM14CC.

TEMPLATE C Cut 3⅜in (8.5cm) strips across the width of the fabric. Each strip will give you 22 triangles per full width. Cut 32 in BM14CC.

BORDER SPACER RECTANGLES Cut 8 rectangles 5½in x 3½in (14cm x 9cm) in BM14CC, these will be trimmed to fit exactly later.

BINDING Cut 9 strips 2½in (6.5cm) across the width of the fabric in GP70BK.

BACKING Cut 2 pieces 40in x 98in (101.5cm x 249cm) in backing fabric.

MAKING THE '4–TRIANGLE' UNITS
Use a ¼in (6mm) seam allowance throughout, it is essential that the seam allowance is accurate and consistent for these units. Refer to the quilt assembly diagram for fabric combinations. The method given will make 2 identical '4–triangle' units from each pair of squares. The Large Squares will make the large '4–triangle' units for the quilt centre blocks and the Small Squares will make the small '4–triangle' units for the pieced border.

Take 2 squares of different fabric, place right sides together matching the edges accurately. Mark a diagonal line from corner

SEWING DIAGRAM

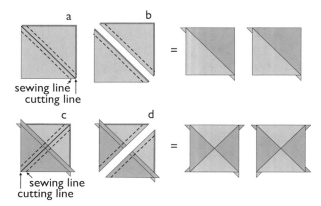

sewing line
cutting line

c

d

=

sewing line
cutting line

CENTRE BLOCK ASSEMBLY DIAGRAM

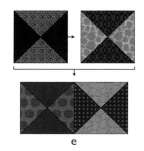

e

CUTTING LAYOUT FOR BM13CC

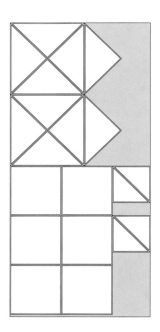

BORDER ASSEMBLY DIAGRAM

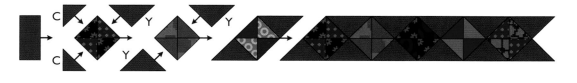

f

g

to corner with a soft pencil or washable marker, this will be the cutting line. Stitch the squares ¹⁄₄in (6mm) from both sides of the cutting line as shown in sewing diagram a.

Cut along the marked cutting line to separate the 2 pieced squares, press the seam allowance towards the darker fabric as shown in sewing diagram b.

Take the 2 pieced squares and place them right sides together matching the seam lines accurately. Mark a diagonal line from corner to corner at right angles to the previous sewing line as shown in sewing diagram c, this will be the cutting line. Stitch the squares ¹⁄₄in (6mm) from both sides of the cutting line as before.

Cut along the marked cutting line to separate the 2 '4–triangle' units, press the seam allowance to one side as shown in sewing diagram d.

Make a total of 48 large'4–triangle' units for the quilt centre blocks and 56 small '4–triangle' units for the pieced border.

MAKING THE BLOCKS

For each centre block (finish to 14in (35.5cm)) take 4 large '4–triangle' units made with large squares. Make 12 blocks as shown in the centre block assembly diagram e.

MAKING THE QUILT CENTRE

Lay out the blocks on point as shown in the

quilt assembly diagram alternating the pieced blocks with the large squares. Add the side setting triangles and corner setting triangles to complete the edges and corners of the centre. Carefully separate into diagonal rows and join. Join the rows to complete the quilt centre.

ADDING THE BORDER

Using the small '4–triangle' units, and the templates Y and C triangles piece 4 borders as shown in border assembly diagram f and 4 corner posts as shown in diagram g. The borders will be shorter than the quilt sides, so stitch a border spacer rectangle to each end of the borders. Trim each border evenly to fit exactly, then add the side borders to the quilt sides. Add a border corner post to each end of the top and bottom borders then add to the quilt centre to complete the quilt.

FINISHING THE QUILT

Press the quilt top. Seam the backing pieces using a ¼in (6mm) seam allowance to form a piece approx. 78in x 98in (198cm x 249cm). Layer the quilt top, batting and backing and baste together (see page 140). Using toning machine quilting thread quilt in the ditch throughout the quilt centre and borders. In the centres of the setting squares quilt 6½in (16.5cm) diameter circles (a small plate can be used as a template), with a pattern of 8 radiating lines from the circle out to the edges of the squares in the form a sunburst design. Repeat half this pattern in the side setting triangles and a quarter pattern in the corner setting triangles. Trim the quilt edges and attach the binding (see page 141).

QUILT ASSEMBLY DIAGRAM

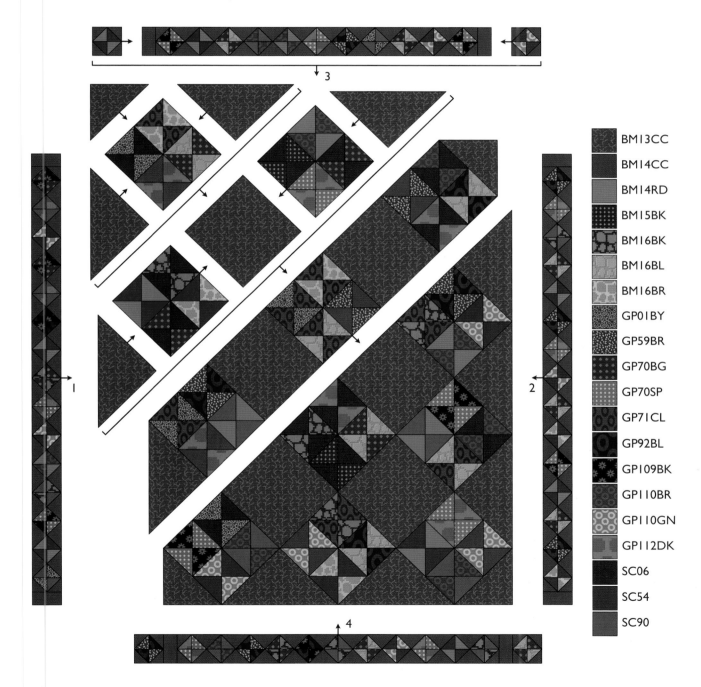

	BM13CC
	BM14CC
	BM14RD
	BM15BK
	BM16BK
	BM16BL
	BM16BR
	GP01BY
	GP59BR
	GP70BG
	GP70SP
	GP71CL
	GP92BL
	GP109BK
	GP110BR
	GP110GN
	GP112DK
	SC06
	SC54
	SC90

crosses ★★★
Kaffe Fassett

We have given Crosses a 3 star rating as setting shapes 'on point' can be fiddly, however the shapes used in this quilt are not hard to handle, just require a little more care. We have specified particular cutting techniques to ensure that the triangles along the pieced block edges do not have bias edges, this makes handling much easier. The full crosses blocks are made using a square (Template T) and 2 triangles (Templates U and V). The blocks are interspaced with sashing strips (cut to size). The row ends are completed with half blocks which are pieced using the same three template shapes as the full blocks. The quilt corners are completed with corner setting triangles (cut to size). The completed quilt centre is trimmed and finally framed with a simple border.

SIZE OF QUILT
The finished quilt will measure approx. 81½in x 81½in (207cm x 207cm).

MATERIALS

PATCHWORK FABRICS
SHELLSCAPE
Red	BM14RD	³⁄₈yd (35cm)

RINGS
Black	BM15BK	½yd (45cm)
Red	BM15RD	¼yd (25cm)

PYTHON
Black	BM16BK	³⁄₈yd (35cm)
Brown	BM16BR	³⁄₈yd (35cm)

ROMAN GLASS
Byzantine	GP01BY	³⁄₈yd (35cm)

GUINEA FLOWER
Brown	GP59BR	¼yd (25cm)

SPOT
Burgundy	GP70BG	¼yd (25cm)

ABORIGINAL DOTS
Chocolate	GP71CL	½yd (45cm)

PLINK
Rust	GP109RU	³⁄₈yd (35cm)

COGS
Brown	GP110BR	³⁄₈yd (35cm)

ROSETTE
Dark	GP112DK	³⁄₈yd (35cm)

SHOT COTTON
Sky	SC62	⁵⁄₈yd (60cm)
Granite	SC66	½yd (45cm)
Pudding	SC68	½yd (45cm)
Aqua	SC77	⁵⁄₈yd (60cm)
Sandstone	SC86	½yd (45cm)
Honeydew	SC95	½yd (45cm)

SASHING, SETTING AND BORDER FABRIC
PLINK
Black	GP109BK	2⁵⁄₈yd (2.4m)

BACKING FABRIC 6¹⁄₈ yd (5.6m)
We suggest these fabrics for backing
PLINK Black, GP109BK
SPOT Burgundy, GP70BG
PYTHON Black, BM16BK

BINDING
SERAPE
Antique	GP111AN	¾yd (70cm)

BATTING
89in x 89in (226cm x 226cm).

QUILTING THREAD
Toning hand quilting threads.

TEMPLATES

T   U   V

CUTTING OUT
We have included a cutting layout for fabric GP109BK and we suggest reviewing it

before cutting this fabric.

BORDERS From the length of the fabric cut 2 borders 2½in x 82½in (6.25cm x 209.5cm) for the quilt top and bottom and 2 borders 2½in x 78½in (6.25cm x 199.5cm) for the quilt sides in GP109BK. These are a little oversized and will be trimmed to fit exactly later.

CORNER SETTING TRIANGLE Cut 2 squares 12in x 12in (30.5cm x 30.5cm) in GP109BK, cut each square diagonally to form 2 triangles. These are a little oversized and will be trimmed to fit exactly later. Total 4 triangles.

SHORT SASHING STRIPS Cut 24 strips 2½in x 11⁷⁄₈in (6.25cm x 30.25cm) in GP109BK.

LONG SASHING STRIPS Cut 40 strips 2½in x 13⁷⁄₈in (6.25cm x 35.25cm) in GP109BK.

TEMPLATE T Cut 2½in (6.25cm) strips across the width of the fabric. Each strip will give you 16 patches per full width. Cut 86 in BM15BK, 73 in GP71CL, 60 in GP01BY, 53 in BM14RD, BM16BK, BM16BR, GP109RU, GP110BR, GP112DK, 46 in GP59BR, 40 in GP70BG, 39 in SC77, 34 in

CUTTING LAYOUT FOR GP109BK

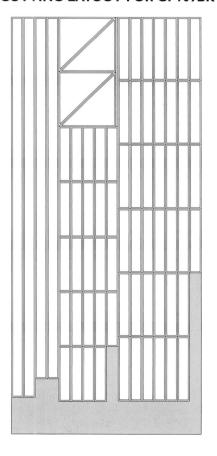

BLOCK ASSEMBLY DIAGRAMS

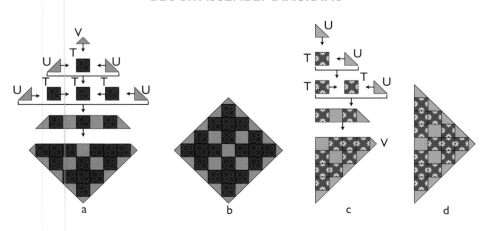

a   b   c   d

SC62, 33 in BM15RD, 26 in SC86, 23 in SC95, 21 in SC66 and 18 in SC68. Total 817 squares.

TEMPLATE U Cut 4in (10.25cm) strips across the width of the fabric. Each strip will give you 40 triangles per full width. Cut 4in (10.25cm) squares, cut each square twice diagonally to form 4 triangles using the template as a guide, this will ensure that the long side of the triangle will not have a bias edge. Note: do not move the patches until both the diagonals have been cut. Cut 96 in SC77, 84 in SC62, 64 in SC86, 56 in SC95, 52 in SC66 and 44 in SC68. Total 396 Triangles. Reserve remaining fabric and trim for Template V.

TEMPLATE V Cut 2¼in (5.75cm) strips across the width of the fabric. Each strip will give you 34 triangles per full width. Cut 27 in SC77, 23 in SC62, 18 in SC86, 17 in SC95, 14 in SC66 and 13 in SC68. Total 112 triangles.

BINDING Cut 9 strips 2½in (6.5cm) across the width of the fabric in GP111AN.

BACKING Cut 2 pieces 40in x 89in (101.5cm x 226cm), 2 pieces 40 in x 10 in (101.5cm x 25.5cm) and 1 piece 10in x 10in (25.5cm x 25.5cm) in backing fabric.

MAKING THE BLOCKS
Use a ¼in (6mm) seam allowance throughout and use the quilt assembly diagram as a guide to fabric placement. Piece 25 full crosses blocks as shown in block assembly diagram a, the finished block can be seen in diagram b. Piece 12 half blocks as shown in diagram c, the finished half block is shown in diagram d.

MAKING THE QUILT
Lay out the blocks in diagonal rows interspacing the blocks with the long and

short sashing strips. Fill in the ends of the rows with the half blocks as shown in the quilt assembly diagram. Piece the rows then join them, adding the corner setting triangles last. You will see that the tips of the sashing along the edges and the corner setting triangles are a little oversized. Trim these flush with the raw edges of the pieced half blocks. Add the side borders trimming to fit exactly and then complete the quilt by adding the top and bottom borders again trimming to fit.

FINISHING THE QUILT
Press the quilt top. Seam the backing pieces using a ¼in (6mm) seam allowance to form a piece approx. 89in x 89in (226cm x 226cm). Layer the quilt top, batting and backing and baste together (see page 140). Using toning hand quilting threads quilt a simple cross hatch pattern across the entire quilt. Trim the quilt edges and attach the binding (see page 141).

QUILT ASSEMBLY DIAGRAM

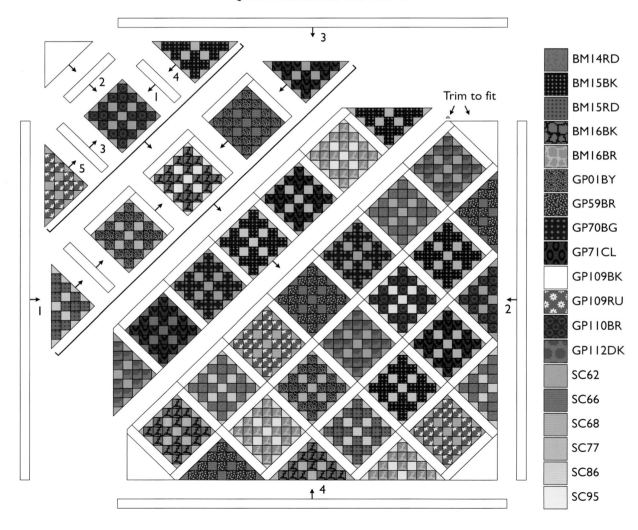

BM14RD
BM15BK
BM15RD
BM16BK
BM16BR
GP01BY
GP59BR
GP70BG
GP71CL
GP109BK
GP109RU
GP110BR
GP112DK
SC62
SC66
SC68
SC77
SC86
SC95

diagonal pathways ★★
Judy Baldwin

The large blocks (finish 12in (30.5cm)) in this quilt are pieced from 4–patch and 9–patch units. Each block is pieced from the same basic selection of fabrics, with the addition of 1 extra feature fabric which gives the finished quilt its distinctive diagonal pattern. The blocks are straight set into rows to form the quilt centre and surrounded by an inner and outer border. The border fabrics should be cut first and the remaining fabric reserved for use in the quilt centre.

SIZE OF QUILT
The finished quilt will measure approx. 87in x 99in (221cm x 251.5cm).

MATERIALS
PATCHWORK AND BORDER FABRICS
LOTUS LEAF
Wine   GP29WN 2yd (1.8m)
PAISLEY JUNGLE
Purple   GP60PU 3/8yd (35cm)
BEKAH
Magenta   GP69MG 2 3/4yd (2.5m)
SPOT
Purple   GP70PU 2 1/2yd (2.3m)
ABORIGINAL DOTS
Cantaloupe   GP71CA 1 1/8yd (1m)
Plum   GP71PL 1/2yd (45cm)
ASIAN CIRCLES
Dark   GP89DK 1/2yd (45cm)
Tomato   GP89TM 1/2yd (45cm)
RADIATION
Red   GP115RD 1/2yd (45cm)
JAPANESE CHRYSANTHEMUMS
Green   PJ41GN 1/2yd (45cm)
IRIS AND PEONY
Magenta   PJ43MG 1/2yd (45cm)

BACKING FABRIC 7 3/4yd (7.1m)
We suggest these fabrics for backing
PAISLEY JUNGLE Purple, GP60PU
RADIATION Red, GP115RD
JAPANESE CHRYSANTHEMUMS Green,
PJ41GN

BINDING
ABORIGINAL DOTS
Plum   GP71PL 7/8yd (80cm)

BATTING
95in x 107in (241cm x 272cm).

QUILTING THREAD
Toning machine quilting thread.

TEMPLATES

CUTTING OUT
Cut the fabric in the order stated to prevent waste.

OUTER BORDERS From the length of the fabric cut 4 borders 6 1/2in x 87in (16.5cm x 222.25cm) in GP69MG. Reserve the remaining fabric for templates Q and J.

TEMPLATE Q Cut 3 1/2in (9cm) strips across the width of the fabric. Each strip will give you 11 patches per full width. Cut 84 in GP70PU, 28 in GP89TM, PJ41GN, 24 in GP89DK, GP115RD, PJ43MG, 20 in GP60PU, 16 in GP69MG and 4 in GP29WN. Total 252 squares. Reserve remaining strips and trim for template J as necessary.

TEMPLATE J Cut 2in (5cm) strips across the width of the fabric. Each strip will give you 20 patches per full width. Cut 504 in GP70PU, 336in GP71CA, 28 in GP89TM, PJ41GN, 24 in GP89DK, GP115RD, PJ43MG, 20 in GP60PU, 16 in GP69MG and 4 in GP29WN. Total 1008 squares.

TEMPLATE X Cut 3 1/2in (9cm) strips across the width of the fabric. Each strip will give you 11 patches per full width. Cut 336 in GP29WN.

INNER BORDER Cut 8 strips 2in (5cm) wide across the width of the fabric in GP71PL. Join as necessary and cut 2 strips 2in x 84 1/2in (5cm x 214.75cm) for the quilt sides and 2 strips 2in x 75 1/2in (5cm x 191.75cm) for the quilt top and bottom.

BINDING Cut 10 strips 2 1/2in (6.5cm) wide across the width of the fabric in GP71PL.

BACKING Cut 2 pieces 40in x 107in (101.5cm x 272cm), 2 pieces 40in x 16in (101.5 x 40.5cm) and 1 piece 28in x 16in (71cm x 40.5cm) in backing fabric.

MAKING THE BLOCKS
Use a 1/4in (6mm) seam allowance throughout and use the quilt assembly diagram as a guide to fabric placement. We have coloured the block assembly diagrams to show the colour of the patches which are always the same. The white patches represent the feature fabric squares which change for each block. For each block piece 4 4–patch units as shown in block assembly diagrams a and b. Next combine the 4–patch units with 4 template Q feature fabric squares (use the same feature fabric throughout the block) as shown in diagrams c and d. Make 2 9–patch units as shown in diagrams e and f. Finally combine the units to complete the block as shown in diagram g. The finished block can be seen in diagram h. Make 42 blocks.

BLOCK ASSEMBLY DIAGRAMS

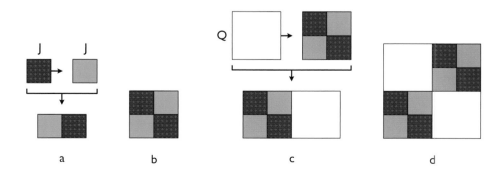

a   b   c   d

MAKING THE QUILT

Lay out the blocks in 7 rows of 6 blocks as shown in the quilt assembly diagram. Check that the diagonal pattern created by the feature fabrics runs consistently throughout the quilt. Piece the rows and then join them to form the quilt centre. Add the side inner borders, then the top and bottom inner borders followed by the side outer borders then the top and bottom outer borders as indicated in the quilt assembly diagram to complete the quilt.

FINISHING THE QUILT

Press the quilt top. Seam the backing pieces using a ¼in (6mm) seam allowance to form a piece approx. 95in x 107in (241cm x 272cm). Layer the quilt top, batting and backing and baste together (see page 140). Using toning machine quilting thread, free motion quilt in a meander pattern across the quilt centre and inner border. In the outer border, free motion quilt following the floral patterns in the fabric. Trim the quilt edges and attach the binding (see page 141).

BLOCK ASSEMBLY DIAGRAMS

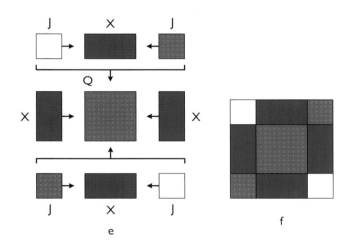

e

f

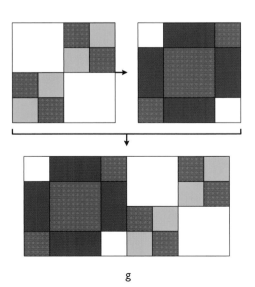

g

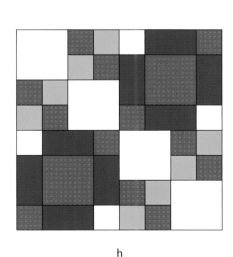

h

QUILT ASSEMBLY DIAGRAM

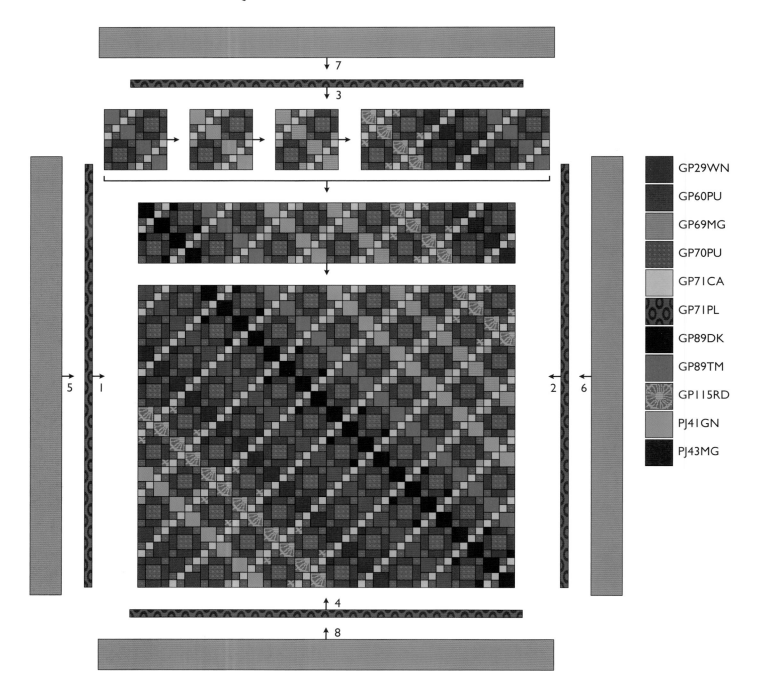

GP29WN
GP60PU
GP69MG
GP70PU
GP71CA
GP71PL
GP89DK
GP89TM
GP115RD
PJ41GN
PJ43MG

reflecting pool ★★
Sally Davis

2 block types (both finish 12in (30.5cm) square) make up this alternating design. The first block is pieced using a rectangle patch shape (Template N). The second block is a framed square, where fussy cut large squares are framed using strips in 'log cabin' style cutting the strips to size as you go. The blocks are straight set into rows to form the quilt centre and surrounded by an inner and outer border.

SIZE OF QUILT

The finished quilt will measure approx. 74in x 98in (188cm x 249cm).

MATERIALS

PATCHWORK FABRICS

BEKAH
Cobalt   GP69CB   ¾yd (70cm)
ABORIGINAL DOTS
Plum   GP71PL   ⅜yd (35cm)
MILLEFIORE
Blue   GP92BL   ¾yd (70cm)
JAPANESE CHRYSANTHEMUM
Green   PJ41GN   5½yd (5m)
SHOT COTTON
Jade   SC41   ⅜yd (35cm)
Cobalt   SC45   ¼yd (25cm)
Aegean   SC46   ¼yd (25cm)
Viridian   SC55   ¼yd (25cm)
Pool   SC71   ¼yd (25cm)
Cactus   SC92   ½yd (45cm)

BACKING FABRIC 7¼yd (6.6m)
We suggest these fabrics for backing
MILLEFIORE Blue, GP92BL
Any of the SHOT COTTONS used in the quilt.

BINDING

JAPANESE CHRYSANTHEMUM
Green   PJ41GN   ¾yd (70cm)

BATTING

82in x 106in (208.5cm x 269cm).

QUILTING THREAD

Toning machine quilting thread.

TEMPLATES

N   Large Square

CUTTING OUT

The Japanese Chrysanthemum fabric, PJ41GN is used for the outer borders, template N and the large squares, which are fussy cut to centre on large blooms. Cut this fabric first in the order stated to prevent waste.

OUTER BORDERS From the length of the fabric cut 2 borders 6½in x 86½in (16.5cm x 219.75cm) for the quilt sides and 2 borders 6½in x 74½in (16.5cm x 189.25cm) for the quilt top and bottom in PJ41GN.

TEMPLATE N (PJ41GN only) From the remaining fabric cut 102 rectangles in PJ41GN.

LARGE SQUARE From the remaining fabric fussy cut 18 squares 10½in x 10½in (26.75cm x 26.75cm) centred on the large blooms in PJ41GN.

TEMPLATE N (other fabrics) Cut 4½in (11.5cm) strips across the width of the fabric. Each strip will give you 11 patches per full width. Cut 54 in GP92BL and 48 in GP69CB.

LOG CABIN FRAMES FOR LARGE SQUARES Cut 1½in (3.75cm) strips across the width of the fabric. Cut 6 strips in GP71PL, SC41, 5 in SC45, SC55, 3 in SC46 and SC71.

INNER BORDER Cut 8 strips 1½in (3.75cm)

wide across the width of the fabric, join as necessary and cut 2 borders 1½in x 84½in (3.75cm x 214.5cm) for the quilt sides and 2 borders 1½in x 62½in (3.75cm x 158.75cm) for the quilt top and bottom in SC92.

BINDING Cut 9 strips 2½in (6.5cm) across the width of the fabric in PJ41GN.

BACKING Cut 2 pieces 40in x 82in (101.5cm x 208.5cm) and 1 piece 27 x 82in (68.5cm x 208.5cm) in backing fabric.

MAKING THE BLOCKS

Use a ¼in (6mm) seam allowance throughout and use the quilt assembly diagram as a guide to fabric placement. Start by piecing a total of 17 rectangle blocks using the template N rectangles as shown in block assembly diagram a, the finished block can be seen in diagram b. Each block uses PJ41GN rectangles combined with 1 other fabric, make 9 using GP92BL and 8 using GP69CB.

Next piece a total of 18 framed square blocks. The strips are added in 'log cabin' style in a clockwise rotation as shown in diagram c, the finished block can be seen in

BLOCK ASSEMBLY DIAGRAMS

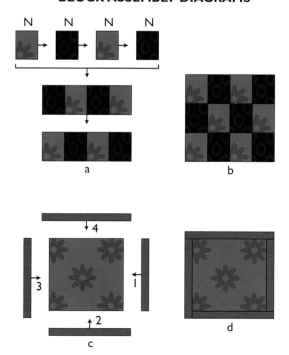

diagram d. Start by laying the first edge of the large square, right sides together, along a Shot Cotton strip. Stitch, press and trim the strip to fit. Rotate the block 90 degrees anti-clockwise and add the next strip in the same manner, again trimming to fit. Repeat for the remaining 2 sides to complete the block.

MAKING THE QUILT
Lay out the blocks in 7 rows of 5 blocks

alternating the pieced rectangle and framed square blocks as shown in the quilt assembly diagram. The pieced rectangle blocks are all placed in the same orientation with 4 rectangles across the top and 3 down the side. Piece the rows and then join them to form the quilt centre. Add the side inner borders, then the top and bottom inner borders followed by the side outer borders and the top and bottom outer borders to complete the quilt.

FINISHING THE QUILT
Press the quilt top. Seam the backing pieces using a ¼in (6mm) seam allowance to form a piece approx. 82in x 106in (208.5cm x 269cm). Layer the quilt top, batting and backing and baste together (see page 140). Using toning machine quilting thread free motion quilt in either a meander style or a floral pattern across the whole quilt surface. Trim the quilt edges and attach the binding (see page 141).

QUILT ASSEMBLY DIAGRAM

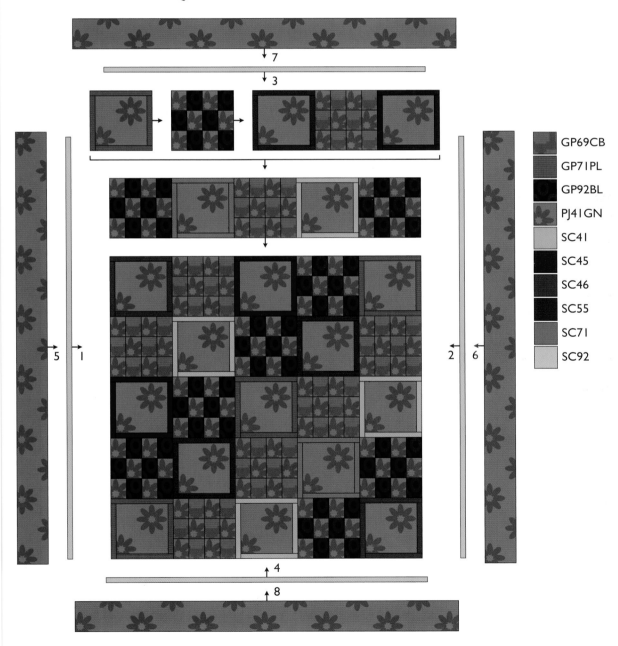

GP69CB
GP71PL
GP92BL
PJ41GN
SC41
SC45
SC46
SC55
SC71
SC92

headlights ★★
Liza Prior Lucy

We have drawn the quilt showing the fabric placement Liza used, however this is meant to be a 'scrappy style' quilt and exact placement of fabrics are not important. 2 block types which finish to 6in (15.25cm) are used, the first block for the quilt centre is pieced from a large and a small triangle patch shape (Templates O and P) and a square patch shape (Template Q). The blocks are straight set into rows. The second block for the pieced border uses the large triangle patch shape from the first block (Template O). We have separated the fabric list into light, dark and accent fabrics. The lights are used for small triangles in the quilt centre and large triangles in the border. The darks are used for the large triangles in the quilt centre and borders and the accent fabrics are used only for the squares in quilt centre blocks.

SIZE OF QUILT
The finished quilt will measure approx. 72in x 84in (183cm x 213.5cm).

> ### TIP BOX
> Liza suggests using a design wall to lay out this quilt, it is the easiest way of ensuring the blocks are turned in the correct orientation to produce the strong diagonal pattern.

MATERIALS
PATCHWORK AND BORDER FABRICS
LIGHT FABRICS
WRINKLE
Black   BM18BK   ½yd (45cm)
HERRINGBONE STRIPE
Blue   BM19BL   ½yd (45cm)
PAPERWEIGHT
Teal   GP20TE   ½yd (45cm)
SPOT
Sapphire   GP70SP   ½yd (45cm)
ASIAN CIRCLES
Dark   GP89DK   ½yd (45cm)
MILLEFIORE
Blue   GP92BL   ½yd (45cm)

DARK FABRICS
DAPPLE
Regal   BM05RE   ⅝yd (60cm)
HERRINGBONE STRIPE
Black   BM19BK   ⅝yd (60cm)
BEADED TENTS
Dark   BM20DK   ⅝yd (60cm)
DANCING PAISLEY
Black   BM22BK   ⅝yd (60cm)
SPOT
Black   GP70BK   ⅝yd (60cm)
ABORIGINAL DOTS
Periwinkle   GP71PE   ⅝yd (60cm)
Plum   GP71PL   ⅝yd (60cm)

ACCENT FABRICS
PAPERWEIGHT
Pumpkin   GP20PN   ¼yd (25cm)
ABORIGINAL DOTS
Ochre   GP71OC   ¼yd (25cm)

ASIAN CIRCLES
Chartreuse   GP89CT   ⅜yd (35cm)
Orange   GP89OR   ¼yd (25cm)
MILLEFIORE
Brown   GP92BR   ¼yd (25cm)
Orange   GP92OR   ¼yd (25cm)

BACKING FABRIC 5½yd (5m)
We suggest these fabrics for backing
MILLEFIORE Blue, GP92BL
BEADED TENTS Dark, BM20DK
DANCING PAISLEY Black, BM22BK

BINDING
HERRINGBONE STRIPE
Black   BM19BK   ¾yd (70cm)

BATTING
80in x 92in (203cm x 233.5cm).

QUILTING THREAD
Ochre and navy blue machine quilting threads.

TEMPLATES

O   P   Q

CUTTING OUT
TEMPLATE O Cut 6⅞in (17.5cm) strips across the width of the fabric. Each strip will give you 10 patches per full width. Cut 26 in BM22BK, 25 in BM19BK, BM25DK, 24 in GP70BK, GP71PL, 22 in BM05RE, GP71PE, 8 in BM18BK, BM19BL, GP20TE, GP70SP, GP89DK and GP92BL. Total 216 triangles. Reserve remaining fabric and trim for template P as necessary.

TEMPLATE P Cut 3⅞in (9.75cm) strips across the width of the fabric. Each strip will give you 20 patches per full width. Cut 42 in BM18BK, BM19BL, GP70SP, 40 in GP92BL, 38 in GP20TE and 36 in GP89DK. Total 240 triangles.

TEMPLATE Q Cut 3½in (9cm) strips across the width of the fabric. Each strip will give you 11 patches per full width, Cut 27 in GP89CT, 20 in GP71OC, GP89OR, 19 in GP92BR, 17 in GP20PN and GP92OR. Total 120 squares.

BINDING Cut 9 strips 2½in (6.5cm) across the width of the fabric in BM19BK.

BACKING Cut 2 pieces 40in x 92in (101.5cm x 233.5) in backing fabric.

MAKING THE QUILT
Use a ¼in (6mm) seam allowance throughout and use the quilt assembly diagram as a guide to fabric placement. Piece 120 blocks for the quilt centre as shown in block assembly diagram a, the finished block can be seen in diagram b. Each block uses a template O triangle in a dark fabric, 2 template P triangles in the same light fabric and a template Q square in an accent fabric. Lay the blocks out as

BLOCK ASSEMBLY DIAGRAM

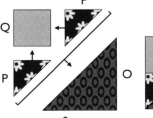
a

b

c

d

shown in the quilt assembly diagram, step back and make sure the orientation of the blocks is correct and the diagonal pattern is consistent. Piece the blocks into 12 rows of 10 blocks, join the rows to complete the quilt centre.

ADDING THE BORDER

Piece 48 blocks for the borders as shown in block assembly diagram c, the finished block is shown in diagram d. Each block uses 2 template O triangles, 1 in a dark fabric and 1 in a light fabric. Lay the blocks out as shown in the quilt assembly diagram making sure that the zig–zag effect runs correctly

around the quilt edge. Piece the blocks into 4 borders and add to the quilt centre as indicated in the quilt assembly diagram.

FINISHING THE QUILT

Press the quilt top. Seam the backing pieces using a $\frac{1}{4}$in (6mm) seam allowance to form a piece approx. 80in x 92in (203cm x 233.5cm). Layer the quilt top, batting and backing and baste together (see page 140). Quilt as shown in the quilting diagram using ochre thread for the accent fabric squares and navy blue thread for the diagonal lines through the large triangles. Trim the quilt edges and attach the binding (see page 141).

QUILTING DIAGRAM

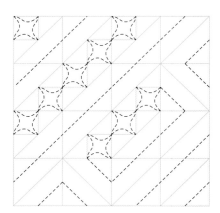

QUILT ASSEMBLY DIAGRAM

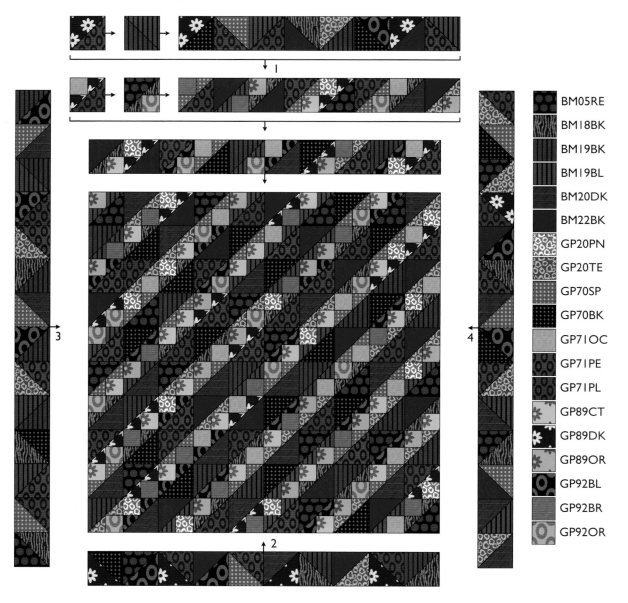

BM05RE
BM18BK
BM19BK
BM19BL
BM20DK
BM22BK
GP20PN
GP20TE
GP70SP
GP70BK
GP71OC
GP71PE
GP71PL
GP89CT
GP89DK
GP89OR
GP92BL
GP92BR
GP92OR

templates

Please refer to the individual instructions for the templates required for each quilt as some templates are used in several projects. The arrows on the templates should be lined up with the straight grain of the fabric, which runs either along the selvedge or at 90 degrees to the selvedge. Following the marked grain lines is important to prevent patches having bias edges along block and quilt edges which can cause distortion. In some quilts the arrows also denote stripe direction.

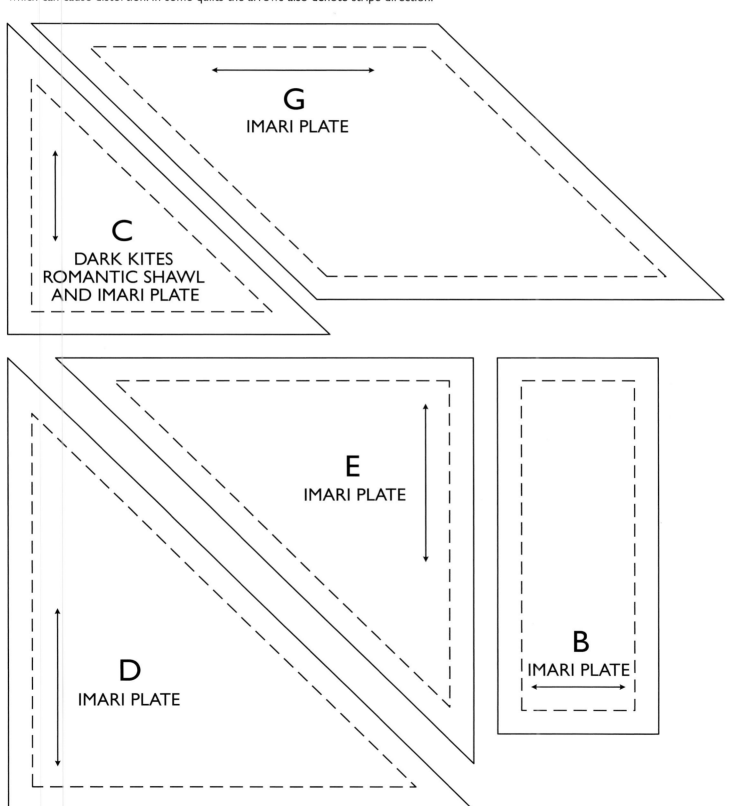

G
IMARI PLATE

C
DARK KITES
ROMANTIC SHAWL
AND IMARI PLATE

E
IMARI PLATE

D
IMARI PLATE

B
IMARI PLATE

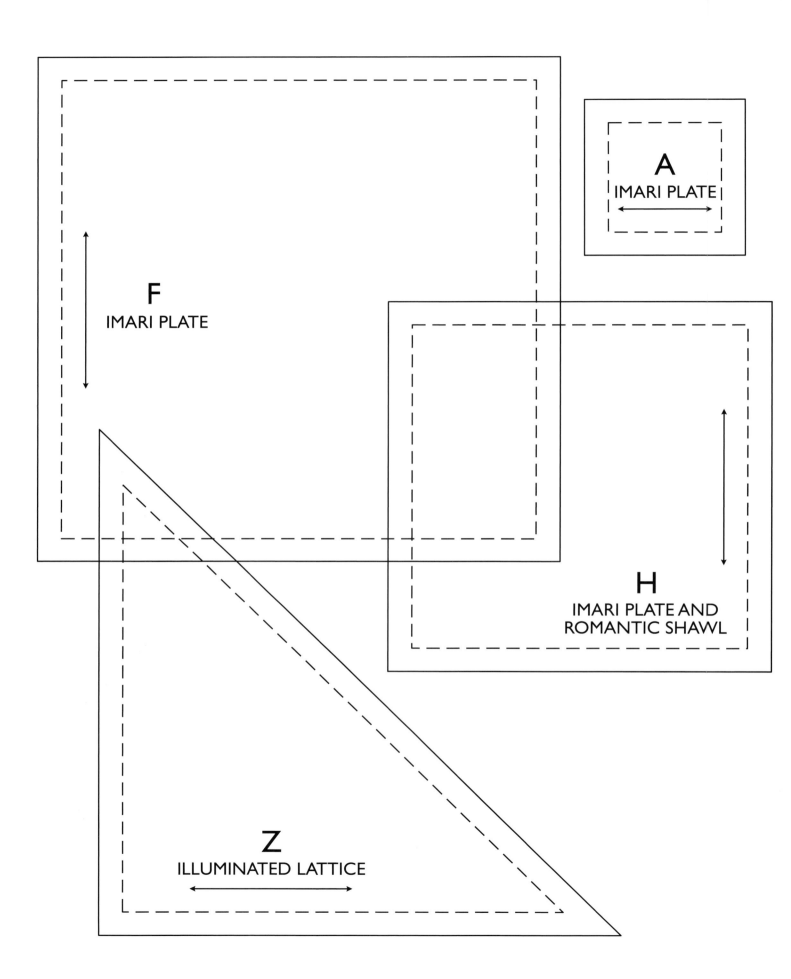

A
IMARI PLATE

F
IMARI PLATE

H
IMARI PLATE AND
ROMANTIC SHAWL

Z
ILLUMINATED LATTICE

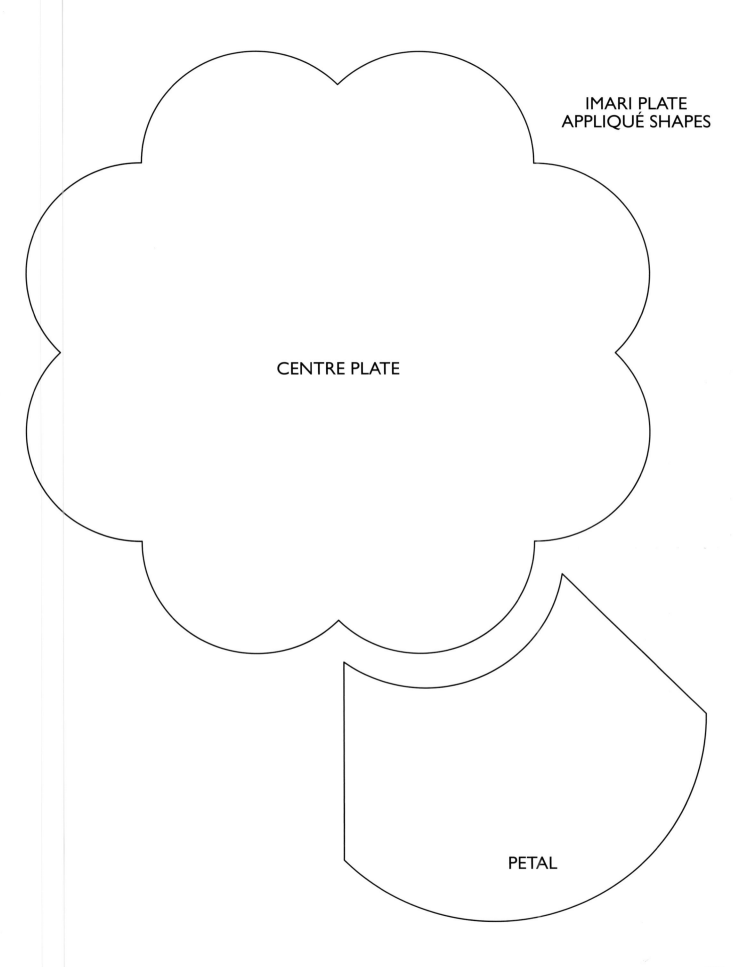

IMARI PLATE
APPLIQUÉ SHAPES

CENTRE PLATE

PETAL

129

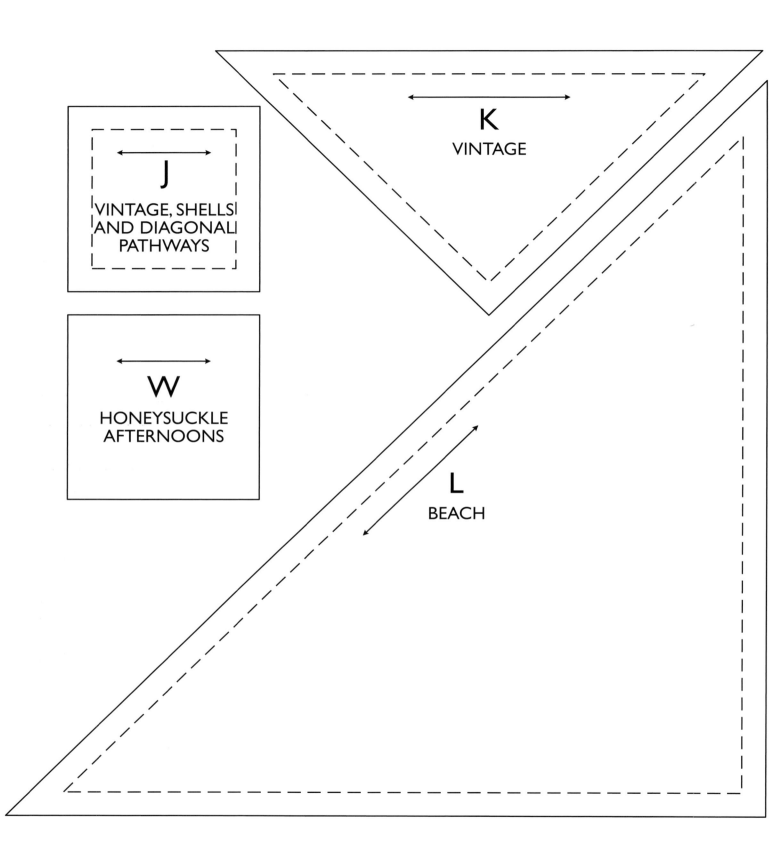

J

VINTAGE, SHELLS
AND DIAGONAL
PATHWAYS

W

HONEYSUCKLE
AFTERNOONS

K

VINTAGE

L

BEACH

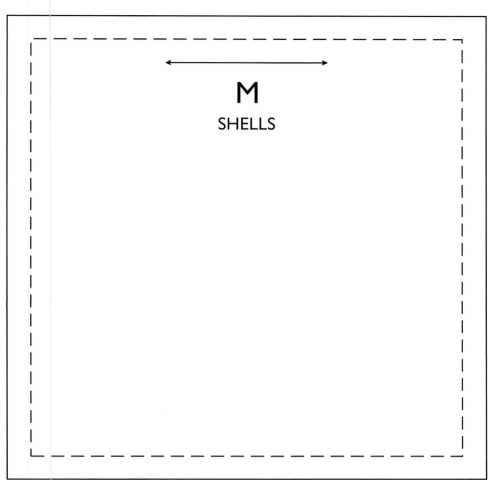

M
SHELLS

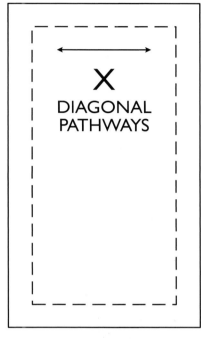

X
DIAGONAL
PATHWAYS

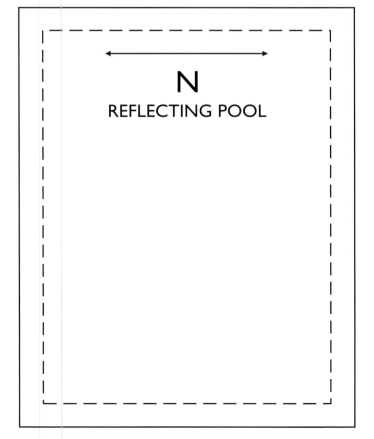

N
REFLECTING POOL

Q
HEADLIGHTS AND
DIAGONAL PATHWAYS

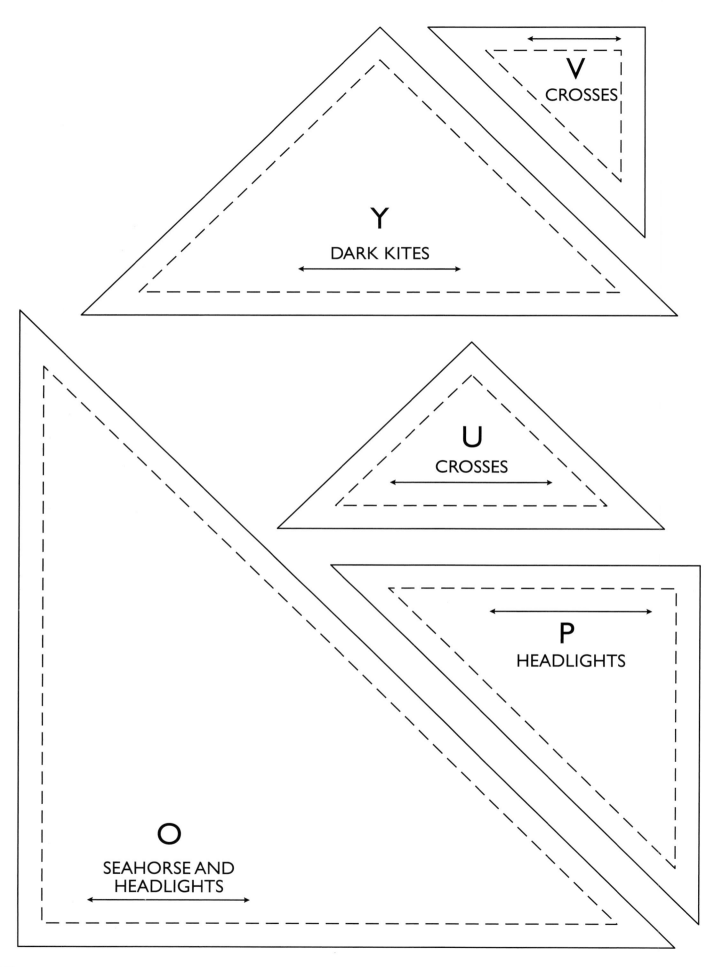

V
CROSSES

Y
DARK KITES

U
CROSSES

P
HEADLIGHTS

O
SEAHORSE AND
HEADLIGHTS

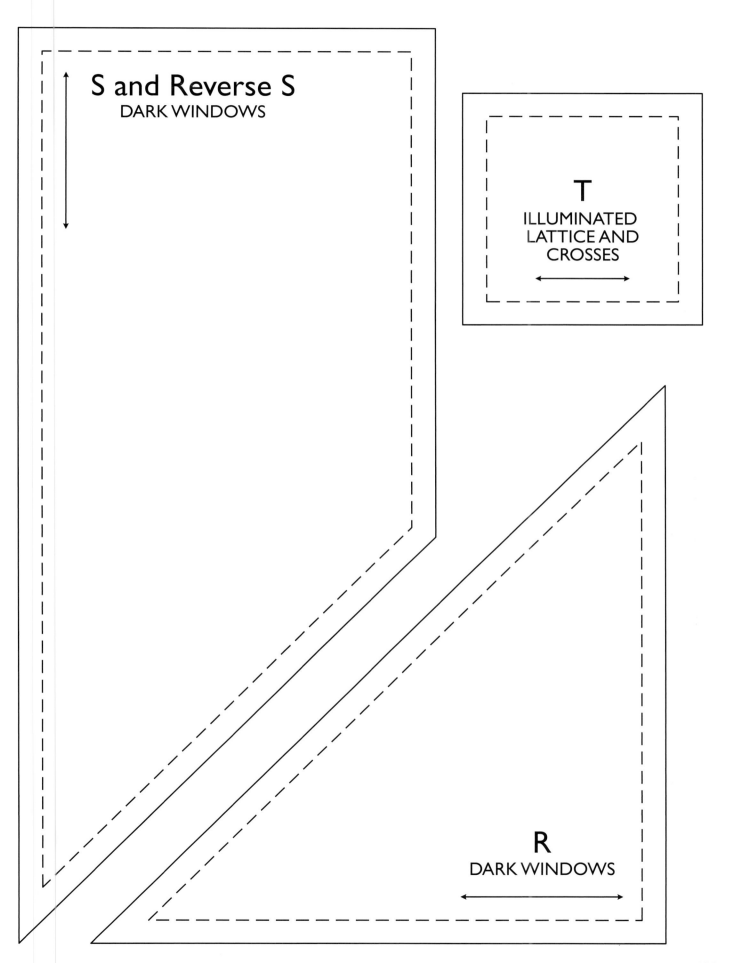

S and Reverse S
DARK WINDOWS

T
ILLUMINATED
LATTICE AND
CROSSES

R
DARK WINDOWS

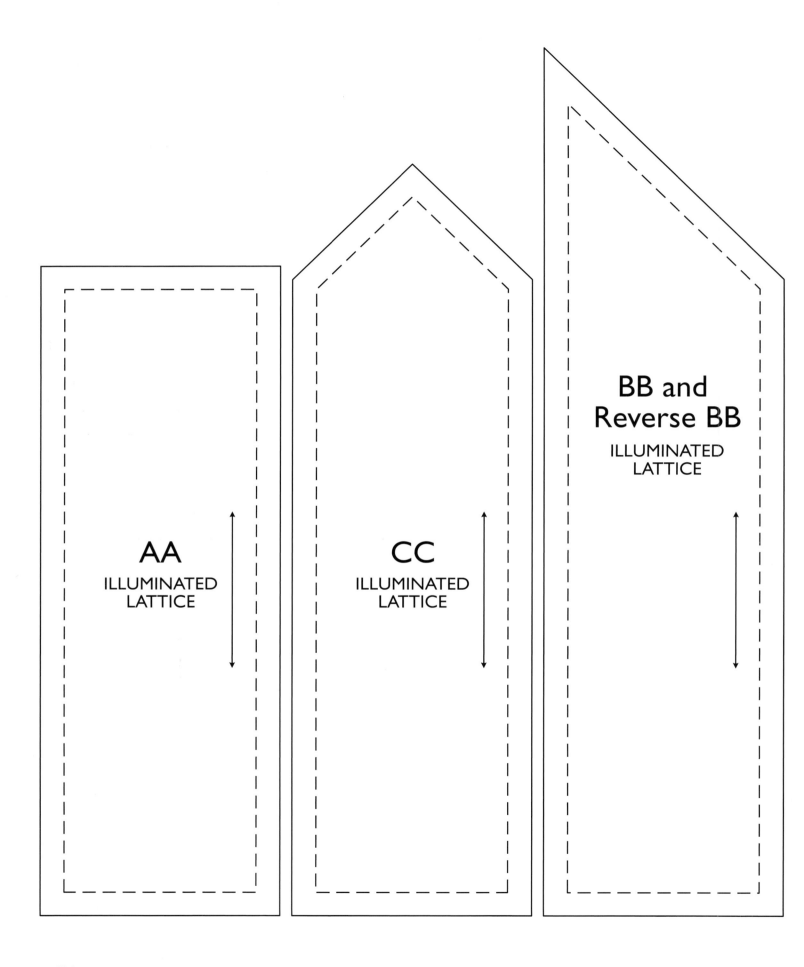

AA
ILLUMINATED
LATTICE

CC
ILLUMINATED
LATTICE

BB and
Reverse BB
ILLUMINATED
LATTICE

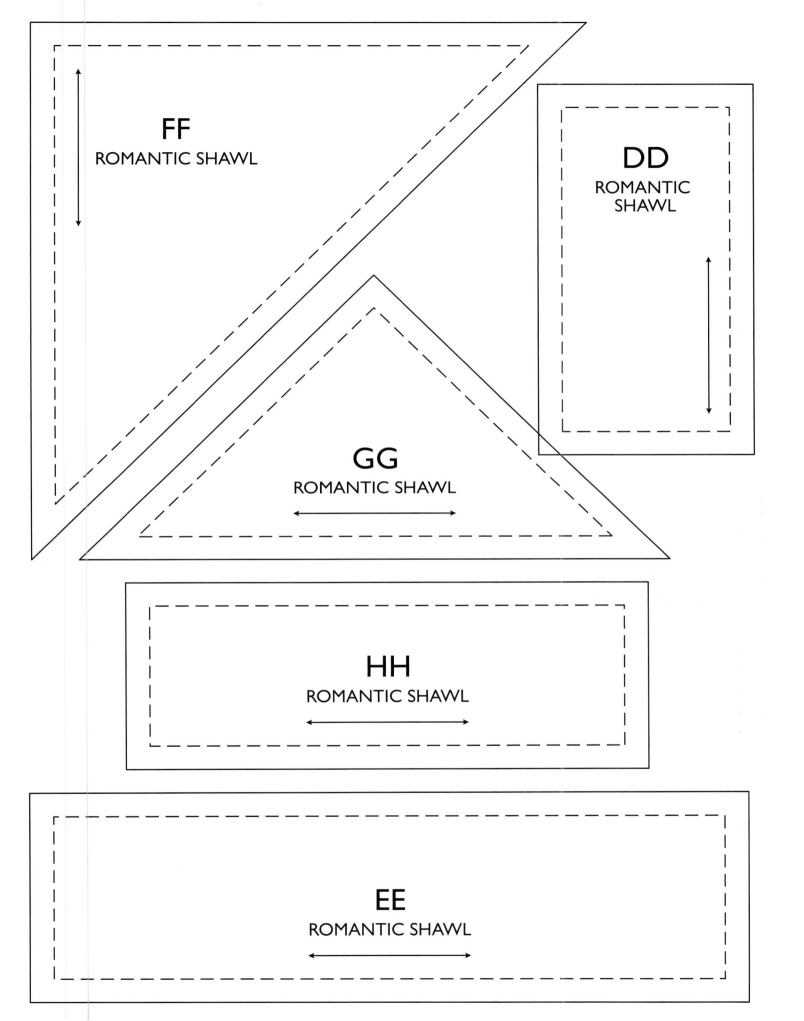

FF
ROMANTIC SHAWL

DD
ROMANTIC
SHAWL

GG
ROMANTIC SHAWL

HH
ROMANTIC SHAWL

EE
ROMANTIC SHAWL

All the templates on this page are printed at 50% of real size. To use, scale up 200% on a photocopier.

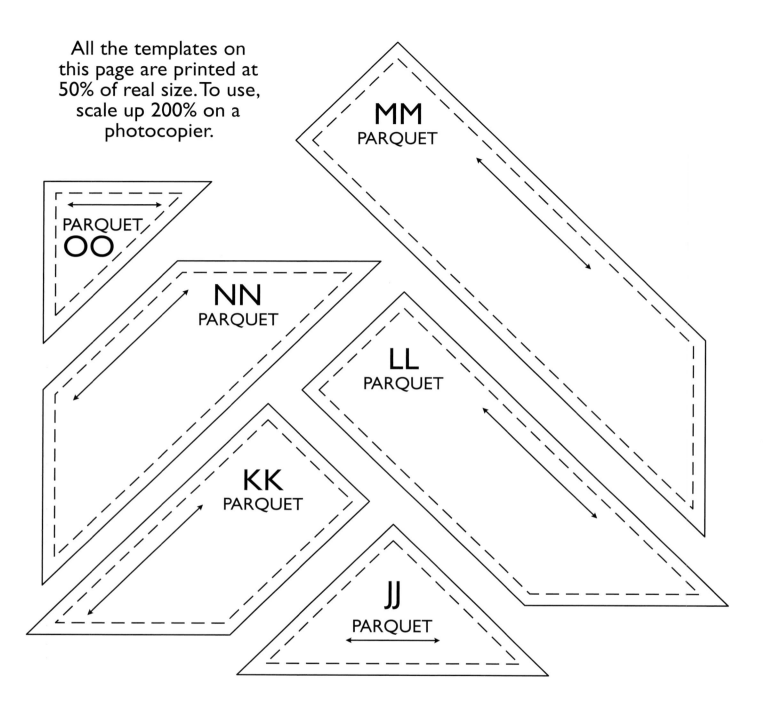

MM
PARQUET

PARQUET
OO

NN
PARQUET

LL
PARQUET

KK
PARQUET

JJ
PARQUET

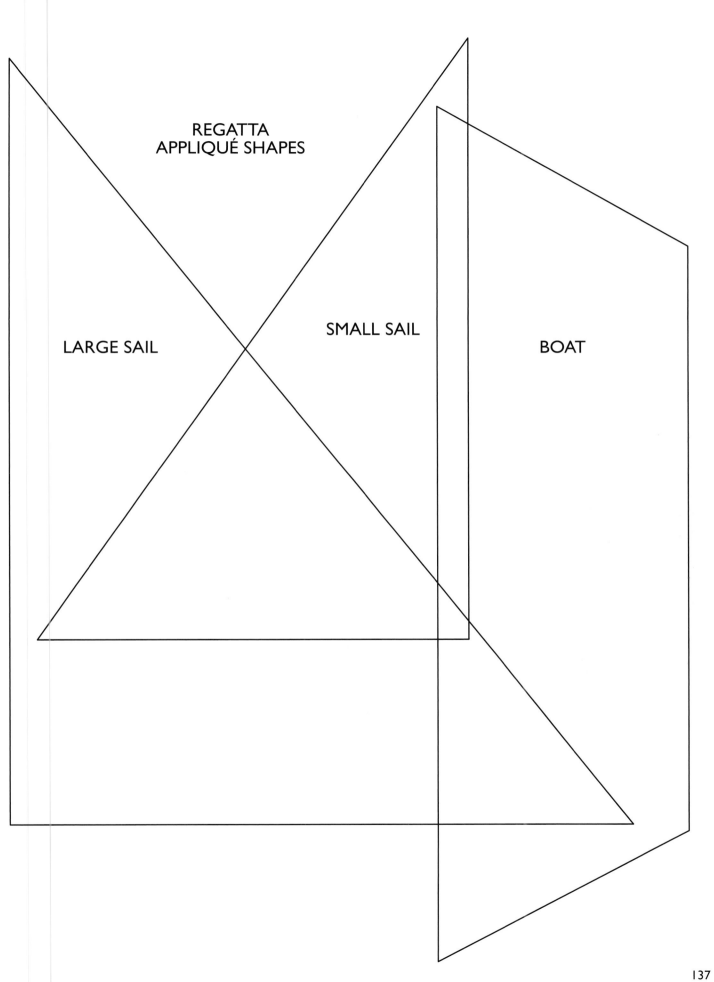

REGATTA
APPLIQUÉ SHAPES

LARGE SAIL

SMALL SAIL

BOAT

patchwork know how

These instructions are intended for the novice quilt maker, providing the basic information needed to make the projects in this book, along with some useful tips.

PREPARING THE FABRIC

Prewash all new fabrics before you begin, to ensure that there will be no uneven shrinkage and no bleeding of colours when the finished quilt is laundered. Press the fabric whilst it is still damp to return crispness to it. All fabric requirements in this book are calculated on a 40in (101.5cm) usable fabric width to allow for shrinkage and selvedge removal.

MAKING TEMPLATES

Transparent template plastic is the best material, it is durable and allows you to see the fabric and select certain motifs. You can also use thin stiff cardboard.

TEMPLATES FOR MACHINE PIECING

1. Trace off the actual–sized template provided either directly on to template plastic, or tracing paper, and then on to thin cardboard. Use a ruler to help you trace off the straight cutting line, dotted seam line and grain lines. Some of the templates in this book were too large to print at full size, they have therefore been printed at half real size. Photocopy them at 200% before using.

2. Cut out the traced off template using a craft knife, ruler and a self–healing cutting mat.

3. Punch holes in the corners of the template, at each point on the seam line, using a hole punch.

TEMPLATES FOR HAND PIECING

• Make a template as for machine piecing, but do not trace off the cutting line. Use the dotted seam line as the outer edge of the template.

• This template allows you to draw the seam lines directly on to the fabric. The seam allowances can then be cut by eye around the patch.

CUTTING THE FABRIC

On the individual instructions for each patchwork, you will find a summary of all the patch shapes used.
Always mark and cut out any border and binding strips first, followed by the largest patch shapes and finally the smallest ones, to make the most efficient use of your fabric. The border and binding strips are best cut using a rotary cutter.

ROTARY CUTTING

Rotary cut strips are usually cut across the fabric from selvedge to selvedge, but some projects may vary, so please read through all the instructions before you start cutting the fabrics.

1. Before beginning to cut, press out any folds or creases in the fabric. If you are cutting a large piece of fabric, you will need to fold it several times to fit the cutting mat. When there is only a single fold, place the fold facing you. If the fabric is too wide to be folded only once, fold it concertina–style until it fits your mat. A small rotary cutter with a sharp blade will cut up to 6 layers of fabric; a large cutter up to 8 layers.

2. To ensure that your cut strips are straight and even, the folds must be placed exactly parallel to the straight edges of the fabric and along a line on the cutting mat.

3. Place a plastic ruler over the raw edge of the fabric, overlapping it about 1/2in (1.25cm). Make sure that the ruler is at right angles to both the straight edges and the fold to ensure that you cut along the straight grain. Press down on the ruler and wheel the cutter away from yourself along the edge of the ruler.

4. Open out the fabric to check the edge. Don't worry if it's not perfectly straight, a little wiggle will not show when the quilt is stitched together. Re–fold fabric, then place the ruler over the trimmed edge, aligning edge with the markings on the ruler that match the correct strip width. Cut strip along the edge of the ruler.

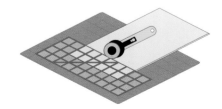

USING TEMPLATES

The most efficient way to cut out templates is by first rotary cutting a strip of fabric the width stated for your template, and then marking off your templates along the strip,

edge to edge at the required angle. This method leaves hardly any waste and gives a random effect to your patches.
A less efficient method is to fussy cut, where the templates are cut individually by placing them on particular motifs or stripes, to create special effects. Although this method is more wasteful it yields very interesting results.

1. Place the template face down, on the wrong side of the fabric, with the grain line arrow following the straight grain of the fabric, if indicated. Be careful though – check with your individual instructions, as some instructions may ask you to cut patches on varying grains.

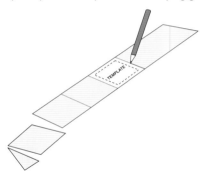

2. Hold the template firmly in place and draw around it with a sharp pencil or crayon, marking in the corner dots or seam lines. To save fabric, position patches close together or even touching. Don't worry if outlines positioned on the straight grain when drawn on striped fabrics do not always match the stripes when cut – this will add a degree of visual excitement to the patchwork!

3. Once you've drawn all the pieces needed, you are ready to cut the fabric, with either a rotary cutter and ruler, or a pair of sharp sewing scissors.

BASIC HAND AND MACHINE PIECING

Patches can be joined together by hand or machine. Machine stitching is quicker, but hand assembly allows you to carry your patches around with you and work on them in every spare moment. The choice is yours. For techniques that are new to you, practise on scrap pieces of fabric until you feel confident.

MACHINE PIECING

Follow the quilt instructions for the order in which to piece the individual patchwork blocks and then assemble the blocks together in rows.

1. Seam lines are not marked on the fabric, so stitch ¼in (6mm) seams using the machine needle plate, a ¼in (6mm) wide machine foot, or tape stuck to the machine as a guide. Pin two patches with right sides together, matching edges.

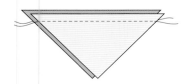

Set your machine at 10–12 stitches per inch (2.5cm) and stitch seams from edge to edge, removing pins as you feed the fabric through the machine.

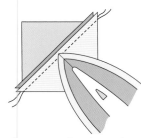

2. Press the seams of each patchwork block to one side before attempting to join it to another block.

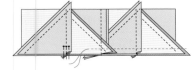

3. When joining rows of blocks, make sure that adjacent seam allowances are pressed in opposite directions to reduce bulk and make matching easier. Pin pieces together directly through the stitch line and to the right and left of the seam. Remove pins as you sew. Continue pressing seams to one side as you work.

HAND PIECING

1. Pin two patches with right sides together, so that the marked seam lines are facing outwards.

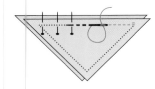

2. Using a single strand of strong thread, secure the corner of a seam line with a couple of back stitches.

3. Sew running stitches along the marked line, working 8–10 stitches per inch (2.5cm) and ending at the opposite seam line corner with a few back stitches. When hand piecing never stitch over the seam allowances.

4. Press the seams to one side, as shown in machine piecing (Step 2).

INSET SEAMS

In some patchwork layouts a patch will have to be sewn into an angled corner formed by the joining of two other patches. Use the following method whether you are machine or hand piecing. Don't be intimidated – this is not hard to do once you have learned a couple of techniques. The seam is sewn from the centre outwards in two halves to ensure that no tucks appear at the centre.

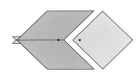

1. Mark with dots exactly where the inset will be joined and mark the seam lines on the wrong side of the fabric on the inset patch.

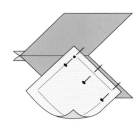

2. With right sides together and inset piece on top, pin through the dots to match the inset points. Pin the rest of the seam at right angles to the stitching line, along one edge of an adjoining patch.

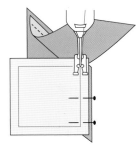

3. Stitch the patch in place along the seam line starting with the needle down through the inset point dots. Secure thread with a backstitch if hand piecing, or stitch forward for a few stitches before backstitching, when machine piecing.

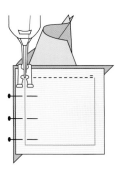

4. Pivot the patch, to enable it to align with the adjacent side of the angled corner, allowing you work on the second half of the seam. Starting with a pin at the inset point once again. Pin and stitch the second side in place, as before. Check seams and press carefully.

HAND APPLIQUÉ

Good preparation is essential for speedy and accurate hand appliqué. The finger–pressing method is suitable for needle–turning application, used for simple shapes like leaves and flowers. Using a card template is the best method for bold simple motifs such as circles.

FINGER–PRESSING

1. To make your template, transfer the appliqué design on to stiff card using carbon paper, and cut out template. Trace around the outline of your appliquéd shape on to the right side of your fabric using a well sharpened pencil. Cut out shapes, adding a ¼in (6mm) seam allowance all around by eye.

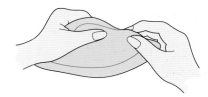

2. Hold shape right side up and fold under the seam, turning along your drawn line, pinch to form a crease. Dampening the fabric makes this very easy. When using shapes with 'points' such as leaves turn the seam allowance at the 'point' in first as shown in the diagram, then continue all round the shape. If your shapes have sharp curves you can snip the seam allowance to ease the curve. Take care not to stretch the appliqué shapes as you work.

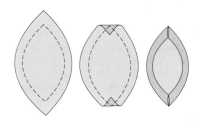

CARD TEMPLATES

1. Cut out appliqué shapes as shown in step 1 of finger–pressing. Make a circular template from thin cardboard, without seam allowances.

2. Using a matching thread, work a row of running stitches close to the edge of the fabric circle. Place thin cardboard template in the centre of the fabric circle on the wrong side of the fabric.

3. Carefully pull up the running stitches to gather up the edge of the fabric circle around the cardboard template. Press, so that no puckers or tucks appear on the right side. Then, carefully pop out the cardboard template without distorting the fabric shape.

FREEZER PAPER

1. Trace the appliqué shape onto the freezer paper and cut out. Make sure the coated side of the paper is next to the fabric and press onto the reverse. Cut out 1/4in (6mm) outside the paper edge. Baste the seam allowance to the reverse, snipping the seam allowance at curves and points will allow it to lay flat.

2. Using a matching thread, bring the needle up from the back of the block into the edge of the shape and proceed to blind–hem in place. This is a stitch where the motifs appear to be held on invisibly. Bring the thread out from below through the folded edge of the motif, never on the top. Work around the complete shape, then turn the block over and remove the backing fabric from behind the appliqué shape leaving a 1/4in (6mm) seam allowance. Remove basting threads and peel off the freezer paper.

NEEDLE–TURNING APPLICATION

1. Take the appliqué shape and pin in position. Stroke the seam allowance under with the tip of the needle as far as the creased pencil line, and

hold securely in place with your thumb. Using a matching thread, bring the needle up from the back of the block into the edge of the shape and proceed to blind–hem in place. This is a stitch where the motifs appear to be held on invisibly. Bring the thread out from below through the folded edge of the motif, never on the top. The stitches must be worked small, even and close together to prevent the seam allowance from unfolding and frayed edges appearing. Try to avoid pulling the stitches too tight, as this will cause the motifs to pucker up. Work around the whole shape, stroking under each small section before sewing.

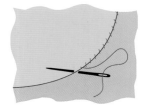

QUILTING AND FINISHING

When you have finished piecing your patchwork and added any borders, press it carefully. It is now ready for quilting.

MARKING QUILTING DESIGNS AND MOTIFS

Many tools are available for marking quilting patterns, check the manufacturer's instructions for use and test on scraps of fabric from your project. Use an acrylic ruler for marking straight lines.

STENCILS

Some designs require stencils, these can be made at home, by transferring the designs on to template plastic, or stiff cardboard. The design is then cut away in the form of long dashes, to act as guides for both internal and external lines. These stencils are a quick method for producing an identical set of repeated designs.

PREPARING THE BACKING AND BATTING

• Remove the selvedges and piece together the backing fabric to form a backing at least 4in (10cm) larger all round than the patchwork top.

• For quilting choose a fairly thin batting, preferably pure cotton, to give your quilt a flat appearance. If your batting has been rolled up, unroll it and let it rest before cutting it to the same size as the backing.

• For a large quilt it may be necessary to join 2 pieces of batting to fit. Lay the pieces of batting on a flat surface so that they overlap by approx. 8in (20cm). Cut a curved line through both layers.

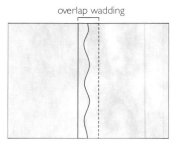
overlap wadding

• Carefully peel away the two narrow pieces and discard. Butt the curved cut edges back together. Stitch the two pieces together using a large herringbone stitch.

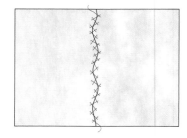

BASTING THE LAYERS TOGETHER

1. On a bare floor or large work surface, lay out the backing with wrong side uppermost. Use weights along the edges to keep it taut.

2. Lay the batting on the backing and smooth it out gently. Next lay the patchwork top, right side up, on top of the batting and smooth gently until there are no wrinkles. Pin at the corners and at the midpoints of each side, close to the edges.

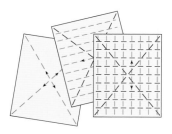

3. Beginning at the centre, baste diagonal lines outwards to the corners, making your stitches about 3in (7.5cm) long. Then, again starting at the centre, baste horizontal and vertical lines out to the edges. Continue basting until you have basted a grid of lines about 4in (10cm) apart over the entire quilt.

4. For speed, when machine quilting, some quilters prefer to baste their quilt sandwich layers together using rust–proof safety pins, spaced at 4in (10cm) intervals over the entire quilt.

HAND QUILTING

This is best done with the quilt mounted on a quilting frame or hoop, but as long as you have basted the quilt well, a frame is not essential. With the quilt top facing upwards, begin at the centre of the quilt and make even running stitches following the design. It is more important to make even stitches on both sides of the quilt than to make small ones. Start and finish your stitching with back stitches and bury the ends of your threads in the batting.

MACHINE QUILTING

• For a flat looking quilt, always use a walking foot on your machine for straight lines, and a darning foot for free–motion quilting.

• It's best to start your quilting at the centre of the quilt and work out towards the borders, doing the straight quilting lines first (stitch–in–the–ditch) followed by the free–motion quilting.

• When free motion quilting stitch in a loose meandering style as shown in the diagrams. Do not stitch too closely as this will make the quilt feel stiff when finished. If you wish you can include floral themes or follow shapes on the printed fabrics for added interest.

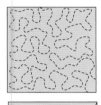

• Make it easier for yourself by handling the quilt properly. Roll up the excess quilt neatly to fit under your sewing machine arm, and use a table, or chair to help support the weight of the quilt that hangs down the other side.

PREPARING TO BIND THE EDGES

Once you have quilted or tied your quilt sandwich together, remove all the basting stitches. Then, baste around the outer edge of the quilt ¼in (6mm) from the edge of the top patchwork layer. Trim the back and batting to the edge of the patchwork and straighten the edge of the patchwork if necessary.

MAKING THE BINDING

1. Cut bias or straight grain strips the width required for your binding, making sure the grainline is running the correct way on your straight grain strips. Cut enough strips until you have the required length to go around the edge of your quilt.

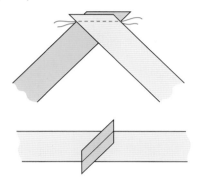

2. To join strips together, the two ends that are to be joined must be cut at a 45 degree angle, as above. Stitch right sides together, trim turnings and press seam open.

BINDING THE EDGES

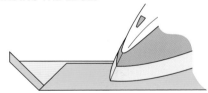

1. Cut the starting end of binding strip at a 45 degree angle, fold a ¼in (6mm) turning to wrong side along cut edge and press in place. With wrong sides together, fold strip in half lengthways, keeping raw edges level, and press.

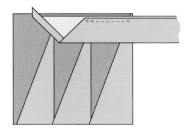

2. Starting at the centre of one of the long edges, place the doubled binding on to the right side of the quilt keeping raw edges level. Stitch the binding in place starting ¼in (6mm) in from the diagonal folded edge (see above). Reverse stitch to secure, and working ¼in (6mm) in from edge of the quilt towards first corner of quilt. Stop ¼in (6mm) in from corner and work a few reverse stitches.

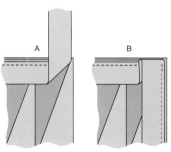

3. Fold the loose end of the binding up, making a 45 degree angle (see A). Keeping the diagonal fold in place, fold the binding back down, aligning the raw edges with the next side of the quilt. Starting at the point where the last stitch ended, stitch down the next side (see B).

4. Continue to stitch the binding in place around all the quilt edges in this way, tucking the finishing end of the binding inside the diagonal starting section (see above).

5. Turn the folded edge of the binding on to the back of the quilt. Hand stitch the folded edge in place just covering binding machine stitches, and folding a mitre at each corner.

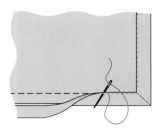

glossary of terms

Adhesive web see fusible web

Appliqué The technique of stitching fabric shapes on to a background to create a design. It can be applied either by hand or machine with a decorative embroidery stitch, such as buttonhole, or satin stitch.

Backing The bottom layer of a quilt sandwich. It is made of fabric pieced to the size of the quilt top with the addition of about 3in (7.5cm) all around to allow for quilting take–up.

Basting or tacking This is a means of holding two fabric layers or the layers of a quilt sandwich together temporarily with large hand stitches, or pins.

Batting or wadding This is the middle layer, or padding in a quilt. It can be made of cotton, wool, silk or synthetic fibres.

Bias The diagonal grain of a fabric. This is the direction which has the most give or stretch, making it ideal for bindings, especially on curved edges.

Binding A narrow strip of fabric used to finish off the edges of quilts or projects; it can be cut on the straight grain of a fabric or on the bias.

Block A single design unit that when stitched together with other blocks create the quilt top. It is most often a square, hexagon, or rectangle, but it can be any shape. It can be pieced or plain.

Border A frame of fabric stitched to the outer edges of the quilt top. Borders can be narrow or wide, pieced or plain. As well as making the quilt larger, they unify the overall design and draw attention to the central area.

Chalk pencils Available in various colours, they are used for marking lines, or spots on fabric.

Cutting mat Designed for use with a rotary cutter, it is made from a special 'self–healing' material that keeps your cutting blade sharp. Cutting mats come in various sizes and are usually marked with a grid to help you line up the edges of fabric and cut out larger pieces.

Design wall Used for laying out fabric patches before sewing. A large wall or folding board covered with flannel fabric or cotton batting in a neutral shade (dull beige or grey work well) will hold fabric in place so that an overall view can be taken of the placement.

Free–motion quilting Curved wavy quilting lines stitched in a random manner. Stitching

diagrams are often given for you to follow as a loose guide.

Freezer paper Paper which is plasticized on one side, usually sold on a roll. Originally used for wrapping meat for freezing it was found to adhere to fabric when pressed. It is useful for appliqué as it stays in place until peeled away without leaving any residue.

Fusible web Adhesive web, which comes attached to a paper backing sheet, used to bond appliqué motifs to a background fabric. There are 2 types of web available, the first keeps the pieces in place whilst they are stitched, the second permanently attaches the pieces so that no sewing is required.

Fussy cutting This is when a template is placed on a particular motif, or stripe, to obtain interesting effects. This method is not as efficient as strip cutting, but yields very interesting results.

Grain The direction in which the threads run in a woven fabric. In a vertical direction it is called the lengthwise grain, which has very little stretch. The horizontal direction, or crosswise grain is slightly stretchy, but diagonally the fabric has a lot of stretch. This grain is called the bias. Wherever possible the grain of a fabric should run in the same direction on a quilt block and borders.

Grain lines These are arrows printed on templates which should be aligned with the fabric grain.

Inset seams or setting–in A patchwork technique whereby one patch (or block) is stitched into a 'V' shape formed by the joining of two other patches (or blocks).

Patch A small shaped piece of fabric used in the making of a patchwork pattern.

Patchwork The technique of stitching small pieces of fabric (patches) together to create a larger piece of fabric, usually forming a design.

Pieced quilt A quilt composed of patches.

Quilting Traditionally done by hand with running stitches, but for speed modern quilts are often stitched by machine. The stitches are sewn through the top, wadding and backing to hold the three layers together. Quilting stitches are usually worked in some form of design, but they can be random.

Quilting hoop Consists of two wooden circular or oval rings with a screw adjuster on the outer

ring. It stabilises the quilt layers, helping to create an even tension.

Rotary cutter A sharp circular blade attached to a handle for quick, accurate cutting. It is a device that can be used to cut up to six layers of fabric at one time. It must be used in conjunction with a 'self–healing' cutting mat and a thick plastic ruler.

Rotary ruler A thick, clear plastic ruler printed with lines that are exactly $\frac{1}{4}$in (6mm) apart. Sometimes they also have diagonal lines printed on, indicating 45 and 60 degree angles. A rotary ruler is used as a guide when cutting out fabric pieces using a rotary cutter.

Sashing A piece or pieced sections of fabric interspaced between blocks.

Sashing posts When blocks have sashing between them the corner squares are known as sashing posts.

Selvedges Also known as selvages, these are the firmly woven edges down each side of a fabric length. Selvedges should be trimmed off before cutting out your fabric, as they are more liable to shrink when the fabric is washed.

Stitch–in–the–ditch or Ditch quilting Also known as quilting–in–the–ditch. The quilting stitches are worked along the actual seam lines, to give a pieced quilt texture.

Template A pattern piece used as a guide for marking and cutting out fabric patches, or marking a quilting, or appliqué design. Usually made from plastic or strong card that can be reused many times. Templates for cutting fabric usually have marked grain lines which should be aligned with the fabric grain.

Threads One hundred percent cotton or cotton–covered polyester is best for hand and machine piecing. Choose a colour that matches your fabric. When sewing different colours and patterns together, choose a medium to light neutral colour, such as grey or ecru. Specialist quilting threads are available for hand and machine quilting.

Walking foot or quilting foot This is a sewing machine foot with dual feed control. It is very helpful when quilting, as the fabric layers are fed evenly from the top and below, reducing the risk of slippage and puckering.

Yo-Yos A circle of fabric double the size of the finished puff is gathered up into a rosette shape.

EXPERIENCE RATINGS

 Easy, straightforward, suitable for a beginner.

 Suitable for the average pachworker and quilter.

For the more experienced patchworker and quilter.

OTHER ROWAN TITLES AVAILABLE

Kaffe Fassett's Country Garden Quilts
Kaffe Fassett's Quilt Romance
Kaffe Fassett's Quilts en Provence

PRINTED FABRICS

When ordering printed fabrics please note the following codes which precede the fabric number and two digit colour code.

GP is the code for the Kaffe Fassett collection

PJ is the code for the Philip Jacobs collection

BM is the code for the Brandon Mably collection

The fabric collection can be viewed online at the following

www.westminsterfibers.com

ACKNOWLEDGEMENTS

We give a huge thank you to Christina Hamnquist, Helene Winberg, Lena Dahrén and all the staff at Skansen Museum for their generosity and help when photographing this book and allowing us unrestricted access.

Skansen is situated on Djurgarden, an island very near Stockholm city centre and is open all year. For more information and opening times check out their website - www.skansen.se/en
Tel: + 46 8442 8000

Rowan 100% cotton premium thread, Anchor embroidery thread, and Prym sewing aids, distributed by Coats Crafts UK, Green Lane Mill, Holmfirth, West Yorkshire, HD9 2DX.
Tel: +44(0) 1484 681881 • Fax +44 (0) 1484 687920

Rowan 100% cotton premium thread and Anchor embroidery thread distributed in the USA by Coats & Clark, 3430 Toringdon Way, Charlotte, North Carolina 28277.
Tel: 704 329 5800 • Fax: 704 329 5027

Prym products distributed in the USA by
Prym-Dritz Corp, 950 Brisack Road, Spartanburg, SC 29303.
Tel: +1 864 576 5050 • Fax: +1 864 587 3353
e-mail: pdmar@teleplex.net

Green Lane Mill, Holmfirth, West Yorkshire, England
Tel: +44 (0) 1484 681881 • Fax: +44 (0) 1484 687920 • Internet: www.knitrowan.com
Email: mail@knitrowan.com

distributors and stockists

Overseas distributors of Rowan fabrics

AUSTRIA
Rhinetex
Geurdeland 7
6673 DR Andelst
The Netherlands
Tel: 31 488 480030
Email: info@rhinetex.com

AUSTRALIA
XLN Fabrics
2/21 Binney Road,
Kings Park
New South Wales 2148
Tel: 61-2 -9621-3066
Email: info@xln.co.zu

BELGIUM
Rhinetex
Geurdeland 7
6673 DR Andelst
The Netherlands
Tel: 31- 488- 480030
Email: info@rhinetex.com

BRAZIL
Coats Corrente Ltd
Rua Do Manifesto,
705 Ipiranga
Sao Paulo
SP 04209-00
Tel: 5511-3247-8000

BULGARIA, GREECE, CYPRUS
Coats Bulgaria EOOD
7 Magnaurska shkola Str.
1784 Sofia, Bulgaria
Tel: +359 2 976 77 41-45
Fax: +359 2 976 77 20
Email: officebg@coats.com
BG: www.coatsbulgaria.bg
GR: www.coatscrafts.gr
CY: www.coatscrafts.com.cy

CANADA
Telio
625 Rue DesLauriers
Montreal, QC, Canada
Tel: 514- 271- 4607
Email: info@telio.com

CZECH REPUBLIC
Coats Czecho s.r.o.
Staré Mesto 246
56932 Staré Mesto
Czech Republic
Tel: 00420 461 616633
Fax: 00420 461 542544
Email: galanterie@coats.com
www.coatscrafts.cz

DENMARK
Coats Expotex AB
Box 297
SE-401 24 Goteborg
Tel: -+46 31 72145-15
Fax: +46 31 471650

FINLAND
Coats Opti Crafts Oy
Ketjutie 3
04220 Kerava
Finland
Tel: 358-9-274871

FRANCE
Rhinetex
Geurdeland 7
6673 DR Andelst
The Netherlands
Tel: 31 488 480 0 30
Email: info@rhinetex.com

GERMANY
Rhinetex
Geurdeland 7
6673 DR Andelst
The Netherlands
Tel: 31 488 480030
Email: info@rhinetex.com

HUNGARY
Coats Crafts Hungary Kft.
H-7500 Nagyatad
Gyar utca 21.
www.coatscrafts.hu

ITALY
Coats Cucirini Srl
Viale Sarca 223
20126 Milano Mi
MILANO

JAPAN
Kiyohara & Co Ltd
4-5-2 Minamikyuhoji-Machi
Chuo-Ku
OSAKA
541-8506
Tel: 81 6 6251 7179

KOREA
Coats Korea Co Ltd,
5F Kuckdong B/D,
935-40 Bangbae-Dong,
Seocho-Gu, Seoul,
South Korea
Tel: 82- 2 -521- 6262

LATVIA
Coats Latvija SIA
Mükusalas iela 41 b
Rïga LV-1004
Latvia
Tel: +371 7 625173
Fax: +371 7 892758
Email: info@coats.lv
www.coatscrafts.lv

LITHUANIA
Coats Lietuva UAB
A.Juozapaviciaus g. 6/2,
LT-09310 Vilinius
Tel: 3705- 2730972
Fax: 3705 2723057
www.coatscrafts.lt

LUXEMBOURG
Rhinetex
Geurdeland 7
6673 DR Andelst
The Netherlands
Tel: 31 488 480 0 30
Email: info@rhinetex.com

NEW ZEALAND
Fabco Limited
280 School Road
P.O. Box 84-002
Westgate
AUCKLAND 1250
Tel: 64- 9- 411- 9996
Email: info@fabco.co.nz

NETHERLANDS
Rhinetex
Geurdeland 7
6673 DR Andelst
The Netherlands
Tel: 31 488 480 0 30
Email: info@rhinetex.com

NORWAY
Coats Expotex AB
Box 297
SE-401 24 Goteborg
Tel: +46 31 7214515
Fax: +46 31 471650

POLAND
Coats Polska Sp.z.o.o
ul. Kaczencowa 16
91-214 Lodz
Tel: 48 42 254 0400
www.coatscrafts.pl

PORTUGAL
Companhia de Linha Coats & Clark, SA
Quinta de Cravel
4430-968 Vila Nova de Gaia
Tel: 00 351- 223 770 700

SINGAPORE
Quilts and Calicos
163 Tanglin Road
03-13 Tanglin Mall
247933
Tel: 65- 688 74708

SLOVAK REPUBLIC
Coats s.r.o.
Kopcianska 94
85101 Bratislava
Slovak Republic
Te: 00421 2 63532314
Fax: 00421 2 63537714
Email: galanteria@coats.com
www.coatscrafts.sk

SOUTH AFRICA
Arthur Bales PTY Ltd
62 4th Avenue
PO Box 44644
Linden 2104
Tel: 27- 11- 888- 2401

SPAIN
Coats Fabra, S.A.
Sant Adria, 20
E-08030 Barcelona
Tel: 00 +34 93- 290. 84. 00
Fax: +34 93-290.84.39

SWITZERLAND
Rhinetex
Geurdeland 7
6673 DR Andelst
The Netherlands
Tel: 31 488 480030
Email: info@rhinetex.com

SWEDEN
Coats Expotex AB
Box 297
SE-401 24 Goteborg
Tel: +46 31 7214515
Fax: +46 31 471650

TAIWAN
Long Teh Trading Co
3F N0 19-2 Kung Yuan Road
Taichung, Taiwan
Tel: 886-4-225-6698

UK
Rowan
Green Lane Mill
Holmfirth
HD9 2DX
United Kingdom
Tel: +44(0) 1484 681881
Email: mail@knitrowan.com
www.knitrowan.com

U.S.A
Westminster Fibers
3430 Toringdon Way
Suite 301,
Charlotte,
NC 28277
Tel: 704-329-5822
Email: fabric@westminsterfibers.com
www.westminsterfibers.com